Gog Magog, and Armageddon
Origins of End Time Battles, Men; and Judgments of God

EDITION 2

Table Content

Introduction
- *The Final Defeat of Satan For All Eternity*
- *Nations Descended from Noah*

Origins of Men and the Influence of Heavenly Beings
- *The origin of Magog*
- *Angels influence the affairs of men*

God Exercises His Authority over all Heavenly Beings and Men
- *The ancient seaport & city of Tyrus*
- *The earthly prince of Tyrus*
- *Satan, the chief prince of high places over Tyrus*

God Speaks to Satan, and to Gog, Descendant of Magog
- *Dispensation (7) of Righteousness & Peace*
- *Prophecy of the Battle of Gog and Magog*
- *Prophecy of the Battle of Armageddon*
- *Ezekiel's Prophecy of the Battle of Armageddon Includes Satan*
- *The prophecy of the Battle of Armageddon Continues*
- *National Israel is Saved and Delivered When They Finally See and Accept Jesus; Messiah*

When Shall These Things Commence to Occur?
- *Daniel Chapter 9 verse 24*
- *Daniel Chapter 9, verses 25 and 26 Explained*
- *Daniel Chapter 9, verse 27 Explained*

End Time Men and Their Authorities
- *Authority of Kingdoms Ruled by Men is Taken Away*
- *The Seventh of the Seven Trumpets Mark the End of Kingdoms Ruled by Men*

Scripture references are from the e-Sword King James Version (KJV) of the Bible.
Illustrations and figures are a combination of Original Content, Internet, and Encyclopedia references.

Preface

Dealing with consequences is part of living, but the average individual is not in the habit of dwelling upon knowing every consequence of their actions; neither do I believe any of us are able to foresee even the simplest of every consequence.

However, I am convinced the Lord God is, and has gone through considerable efforts to ensure the human race know the consequences of those things that would permanently harm us. Thus, the promise of *"John 3:16"* is given for even the most destructive consequence that could come upon us! But the people of the chosen nation of the LORD God have not yet embraced this promise.

And so, now the dilemma exists where Almighty God promised Himself, even from the time of Old Testament prophecies, that He would save the remnant of Israel for Himself. The promise He made Himself includes the bold prophecy that Israel shall remain forever! I believe the prophecy of Gog and Magog to be that final demonstration from God that will convince this, *"remnant of Israel"* of their salvation in Christ Jesus, when he saves them from destructions at the hand of world armies in the Battle of Armageddon, and from Gog of Magog!

Introduction

This study traces prophecies and revealed events that culminate in the two greatest battles that shall ever be known of human kind; the *Battle of Armageddon at the return of Jesus*, and the *Battle of Gog and Magog at the time Satan shall be cast into the lake of fire and brimstone (Revelation 20:7 through 20:10 below).*

The Final Defeat of Satan For All Eternity

Rev 20:7 And when the thousand *(1000)* years are expired *(or Dispensation (7) of Righteousness & Peace (See "Dispensations" in "Definitions & Figures" section; and associated timeline graphics provided))*; Satan shall be loosed out of his thousand year imprisonment,

Rev 20:8 And shall go out to deceive the nations which are in the four quarters of the earth, Gog and Magog, to gather them together to battle: the number of whom *is* as the sand of the sea.

Rev 20:9 And they went up on the breadth of the earth, and compassed the camp of the saints about, and the beloved city: and fire came down from God out of heaven, and devoured them.

Rev 20:10 And the devil that deceived them was cast into the lake of fire and brimstone, where the beast and the false prophet *are,* and shall be tormented day and night for ever and ever.

Our study begins with considering *Genesis 10:1 through 10:5* below; *Ezekiel Chapters 38 & 39, and Revelation 20:7 through 20:10* as shown above for foundational scriptures.

Nations Descended from Noah

Gen 10:1 Now these *are* the generations of the sons of Noah, Shem, Ham, and Japheth: and unto them were sons born after the flood.

Gen 10:2 The sons of Japheth; Gomer, and Magog, and Madai, and Javan, and Tubal, and Meshech, and Tiras.

Gen 10:3 And the sons of Gomer; Ashkenaz, and Riphath, and Togarmah.

Gen 10:4 And the sons of Javan; Elishah, and Tarshish, Kittim, and

Dodanim.

Gen 10:5 By these were the isles of the Gentiles divided in their lands; every one after his tongue, after their families, in their nations.

Sometimes it is useful to look-up any historical records about a difficult topic related to a Bible study. This helps one to gain insight about what has already occurred in Bible prophecy, and it makes following the Bible study easier. So with that in mind, several historical references related to **Gog and Magog** outside of the Bible were investigated before attempting this study. It seems that almost every reference investigated may have borrowed the names "Gog" and "Magog" from Bible Scripture to explain some secular mythical tale. This did not provide much additional insight into this study. Consequently, the only none – Biblical references of those investigated, that we shall be considering for this study, is this: ***"Those that study the migration of people, or family groups, have determined that the offspring of Japheth of Genesis 10:2 migrated and settled in countries north of Israel, and in areas about the Black Sea"***.

The importance of this bit of information is that the prophecy of ***Ezekiel Chapter 38:15*** says that Israel shall be attacked by those ***"from thy place out of the north parts"***. This will become even clearer as we progress in this study. Also, it is believed that other scriptures in the Book of Genesis may help to validate the particular notion that, ***"descendants of Japheth did indeed settle in countries north of Israel"***.

The prophecy in ***Ezekiel Chapter 38*** is directed at an earthly ruler referred to as "Gog". But we should realize that God is also addressing the prince in high places that influences this ruler Gog, and the people "Magog". The chief prince in high places is Satan! And we know from scripture that Satan, and often times one appointed of Satan, takes an active role in orchestrating influence over earthly rulers such as "Gog", ruler of Magog. Thus, there are passages of Scripture where God addresses Gog and Satan as one in the same individual. But, the earthly prince ***(King, or ruler),*** "Gog" is a descendent of Magog, who is introduced in *Genesis 10:2*, and is a son of Japheth *(son of Noah)*.

Similar instances of these kind of "affairs of men being influenced of heavenly creatures" that occurs in *Ezekiel 38* are also seen in *Daniel 10:12 and 10:13, Daniel 10:20, and Ezekiel Chapter 27 through Chapter 28:19;* where it is revealed that spirits in high places are constantly involved in influencing the outcome of human events, through earthly leaders and their peoples, or subjects. Therefore, it seems reasonable that we should be able to gain additional insight into *Ezekiel Chapter 38* by looking at these other scriptures *(Daniel 10:12 and 10:13, Daniel 10:20, and Ezekiel 27 & 28).* Thus, we plan to draw parallels between these scriptures and *Ezekiel Chapter 38* as we develop this study.

Origins of Men and the Influence of Heavenly Beings

The origin of Magog

Now these *are* the generations of the sons of Noah, Shem, Ham, and
Japheth: and unto them were sons born after the flood.
The sons of Japheth; Gomer, and Magog, and Madai, and Javan, and
Tubal, and Meshech, and Tiras.
And the sons of Gomer; Ashkenaz, and Riphath, and Togarmah.
And the sons of Javan; Elishah, and Tarshish, Kittim, and Dodanim.
By these were the isles of the Gentiles divided in their lands; every
one after his tongue, after their families, in their nations.

Genesis 10:1 through 10:5

The first reference to Magog is in *Genesis 10:2*. Included along with
this reference to Magog are Meshech, Tubal, Gomer, Togarmath,
and Tarshish. We also see these same names in *Ezekiel Chapter 38*.
But *"Gog"* is not among them here in Genesis. It is not until *Ezekiel
38, and Revelation 20 verse 8* that the scriptures associate *Magog
with Gog!*

Angels influence the affairs of men

Daniel 10:12 and 10:13, and *Daniel 10:20* is the situation where
Daniel had been praying and fasting for his people Israel until an
angel from God came in answer to his prayers. The angel said he had
been sent from the beginning of Daniel's prayer, twenty-one *(21)*
days earlier. But the prince of Persia hindered him. Now, the prince
that hindered the answer to Daniel's prayer was not an earthly prince,
but a fallen angel from Satan, that was influencing the earthly prince
and affairs of Persia.

Notice also, that the angel from God did not complete his mission of
answering Daniel's prayer until Michael came to help him fight
against the prince of Persia. Then, even after he had delivered the
answer to Daniel's prayer, he returned to fight with the prince of
Persia so that the prince of Grecia *(or Greece, which was Alexander
the Great)* could come to power.

Then said he unto me, Fear not, Daniel: for from the first day that
thou didst set thine heart to understand, and to chasten thyself
before thy God, thy words were heard, and I am come for thy
words.
But the prince of the kingdom of Persia withstood me one and
twenty days: but, lo, Michael, one of the chief princes, came to
help me; and I remained there with the kings of Persia *(or
Michael remained there to fight in my place)*.

Then said he, Knowest thou wherefore I come unto thee? and now
will I return to fight with the prince of Persia: and when I am
gone forth, lo, the prince of Grecia shall come *(to power)*.

Daniel 10:12 through 10:20

As we read the remaining verse of **Daniel Chapter 10**, continuing
into **Daniel Chapter 11**, and then concluding in **Daniel Chapter 12**,
we see the answer to Daniel's prayer revealed. But that is another
Bible study, and we will not attempt to discuss it here, because it is
quiet lengthy.

I believe we have made the case that Satan and his angles are always
attempting to influence an evil outcome to human affairs.
Be sober, be vigilant; because your adversary the devil, as a roaring
lion, walketh about, seeking whom he may devour:

1 Peter 5:8

God exercises his authority over all heavenly beings and men

In *Ezekiel Chapter 27 & 28* God addresses the ancient seaport of Tyrus because of its pride. And yet we know that the place *"Tyrus"* can have no pride except that seen in its inhabitants. Thus, the place is assigned the human traits and identity of those in charge. Now, our first assumption is that God is speaking to the earthly leader of Tyrus about his pride. But then, reading further, we realize that God is speaking to someone even beyond the earthly king of Tyrus. The other individual God is addressing is Satan! Let's just look at a few scriptures concerning this observation:

The ancient seaport & city of Tyrus
The word of the LORD came again unto me, saying,
Now, thou son of man, take up a lamentation for Tyrus;
And say unto Tyrus, O thou that art situate at the entry of the sea,
    which art a merchant of the people for many isles, Thus saith the
    Lord GOD; O Tyrus, thou hast said, I *am* of perfect beauty.
Thy borders *are* in the midst of the seas, thy builders have perfected
    thy beauty.
    ***This scripture seem to also speak of the fact that God created
    Satan perfect; but Satan corrupted himself in so much self
    pride, that his heart exalted him even above God, his creator!***

Ezekiel 27:1 through 27:4

The earthly prince of Tyrus
Son of man, say unto the prince of Tyrus, Thus saith the Lord GOD;
    Because thine heart *is* lifted up, and thou hast said, I *am* a God, I
    sit *in* the seat of God, in the midst of the seas; yet thou *art* a man
    (created of God), and not God, though thou set thine heart as the
    heart of God:
Behold, thou *(Satan)* *art* wiser than Daniel; there is no secret that
    they *(creatures)* can hide from thee:
With thy wisdom and with thine understanding thou hast gotten thee
    riches, and hast gotten gold and silver into thy treasures:
By thy great wisdom *and* by thy traffick *(trade)* hast thou increased
    thy riches, and thine heart is lifted up because of thy riches

(merchandise):
Therefore thus saith the Lord GOD; Because thou hast set thine heart
as the heart of God;
Behold, therefore I *(Lord GOD)* will bring strangers upon thee, the
terrible of the nations: and they shall draw their swords against
the beauty of thy wisdom, and they shall defile thy brightness.
They *(strangers)* shall bring thee down to the pit, and thou shalt die
the deaths of *them that are* slain in the midst of the seas.

Ezekiel 28:2 through 28:8

Satan, the chief prince of high places over Tyrus

Son of man, take up a lamentation upon the king of Tyrus, and say
unto him, Thus saith the Lord GOD; Thou sealest up the sum,
full of wisdom, and perfect in beauty *(In other words according
to Ezekiel 28:12 and 13, the Lord GOD says I put these
qualities and merchandise in you)*.
Thou hast been in Eden the garden of God; every precious stone *was*
thy covering, the sardius, topaz, and the diamond, the beryl, the
onyx, and the jasper, the sapphire, the emerald, and the
carbuncle, and gold: the workmanship of thy tabrets and of thy
pipes was prepared in thee in the day that thou wast created.
Thou *art* the anointed cherub that covereth; and I have set thee *so*:
thou wast upon the holy mountain of God; thou hast walked up
and down in the midst of the stones of fire. *(While I have no
evidence that this word, "covereth" translates into "covet", I
think it is worth mentioning that God created Satan the
anointed cherub, but he became covetous in his corrupt pride?
The most abominable covetousness of Satan was that he
purposed to be in the place of God)*
Thou *(Lucifer)* *wast* perfect in thy ways from the day that thou wast
created, till iniquity was found in thee *(who has become corrupt and
is now Satan; the devil. But God did not create him corrupt;
neither did God create Adam with sin)*.

Ezekiel 28:12 through 28:15

*Just as all the qualities and merchandise the LORD God used to
create Lucifer in Ezekiel 28:12 and 28:13 eventually became more
important in the heart and eyes of Lucifer than God his creator,*

the ancient seaport of Tyrus also stumbled in the same manner of self pride concerning the beauty and merchandise of her trafficking, or trading.
And I must say today, the visible Church struggles with these very same things, while world societies are preoccupied with (committed to) their merchandise in their actions of rejecting God.
Now we see our laws have legalized rejection of God and salvation by Christ Jesus, which has resulted in the God of Creation becoming increasingly "irrelevant" to the world. Thus, since the world has rejected God, the second coming of the Lord Jesus shall not be to save the world, but to save the people of God out of the world (study the Book of Revelation)!

By the multitude of thy merchandise they *(thy merchandise)* have filled the midst of thee with violence, and thou hast sinned *(defied the authority of Almighty God, and not repented)*: therefore I will cast thee as profane out of the mountain of God: and I will destroy thee, O covering cherub, from the midst of the stones of fire.

Thine heart was lifted up because of thy beauty, thou hast corrupted thy wisdom by reason of thy brightness: I will cast thee to the ground, I will lay thee before kings *(saints, redeemed men)*, that they may behold thee.

Thou hast defiled thy sanctuaries *uniqueness/ holiness?)* by the multitude of thine iniquities, by the iniquity of thy traffick *(trading merchandise, or stuff?)*; therefore will I bring forth a fire from the midst of thee, it shall devour thee, and I will bring thee to ashes upon the earth in the sight of all them that behold thee.

All they that know thee among the people shall be astonished at thee: thou shalt be a terror, and never *shalt* thou *be* any more.

Ezekiel 28:18 and 28:19

Isaiah Chapter 14 is another series of scripture that comes to mind, which is written in the same manner as *Ezekiel Chapters 27 & 28*. In this situation God begins by addressing the earthly king of Babylon, and then Satan. Let's take a look.

And it shall come to pass in the day that the LORD shall give thee
(Israel) rest from thy sorrow, and from thy fear, and from the
hard bondage wherein thou wast made to serve,
That thou shalt take up this proverb against the king of Babylon, and
say, How hath the oppressor ceased! the golden city ceased!
The LORD hath broken the staff of the wicked, *and* the sceptre of
the rulers *(of men)*.
He *(wicked ruler)* who smote the people in wrath with a continual
stroke, he that ruled the nations in anger, is persecuted, *and* none
hindereth *(or aided him)*.
The whole earth is at rest, *and* is quiet: they *(the whole earth)* break
forth into singing.
Yea, the fir trees rejoice at thee, *and* the cedars of Lebanon, *saying*,
Since thou *(the wicked)* art laid down, no feller is come up
against us. *(I am persuaded this prophecy could also points to
the time of the 1000 years of Righteousness & Peaceful reign
of Jesus when Satan is bound in the bottomless pit. See
scriptures beginning at Revelation 20:1; and Dispensation (7)
of Righteousness & Peace under paragraph, "Dispensations"
in the "Definitions & Figures" section; associated timeline
graphics are also provided).*

Isaiah 14:3 through 14:8

***These next scriptures (Isaiah 14:9 through 14:15) are no longer
just talking about Babylon alone, but Lucifer also***
Hell from beneath is moved for thee to meet *thee* at thy coming: it
stirreth up the dead for thee, *even* all the chief ones of the earth;
it *(hell)* hath raised up from their thrones all the kings of the
nations. . *(The second resurrection; verses 20:5 & 6 of The
Book of Revelation)*
All they shall speak and say unto thee, Art thou also become weak as
we? art thou become like unto us?
Thy pomp is brought down to the grave, *and* the noise of thy viols
(failed musical ability): the worm is spread under thee, and the
worms cover thee.
How art thou fallen from heaven, O Lucifer, son of the morning!
how art thou cut down to the ground, which didst weaken the
nations!

For thou hast said in thine heart, I will ascend into heaven, I will
    exalt my throne above the stars of God: I will sit also upon the
    mount of the congregation, in the sides of the north:
I will ascend above the heights of the clouds; I will be like the most
    High.
Yet thou shalt be brought down to hell, to the sides of the pit.

Isaiah 14:9 – 14:15

I am persuaded that Ezekiel Chapter 38 is similar to these scriptures
(Ezekiel Chapter 27 through 28, and Isaiah Chapter 14) in that these
prophecies are for Satan and his angles as well as earthly rulers. We
already know that the evils of the world are not confined to the
devices of men, but are fueled by Satan and his angles, constantly
working to cause an evil outcome of human events. This is
especially true where evil is done against those that have the favor of
God in Jesus Christ.

Satan is an enemy of God. Therefore, he is always against those God
chooses. This satanic behavior in men will result in the situation
prophesied of in Ezekiel Chapters 38 through 39; especially stirred
up and kindled in the ruler Gog, and the *land; "and\ or attitude"* of
Magog, against ***Israel and the people of God saved out of the
Gentile world!.***

God speaks to Satan, and to Gog, descendant of Magog

This prophecy of Ezekiel's Gog and Magog seems to point to the season when the LORD makes preparation for the Millennial, or Thousand (1000) Years of His Righteous & Peaceful reign! We have referred to it in other studies as, "Dispensation (7) of Righteousness & Peace" (See the paragraph, "Dispensations" in the "Definitions & Figures" section; associated timeline graphics are also provided).

It also seems these years just prior to Dispensation (7) are when Daniel's final (½ week, or 3 1/2 years) is fulfilled with the reconstituted National State of Israel, since 1948 A.D.; (the remnant, "Judah of Israel")!

Beginning in Ezekiel Chapter 38 the *(Holy)* Spirit of God inspires the prophet Ezekiel to prophecy against the earthly king Gog, whom Satan shall use in his efforts to destroy the **people of God**, at or round about **the Battle of Armageddon** *(which is also the same time(s) (and\ or season(s)) described in Revelation 11:15 through 11:19, Revelation 16:16, Revelation 19:11 through 19:21, Zechariah 14)*.

Thus, when God speaks to Gog, *land\ army\ attitude* of Magog *(descendants of Genesis 10:2 Magog)*, he is speaking to Satan also. We make this assessment because Satan go about the earth with this very same purpose in his heart to destroy the people of God after the thousand year reign of Christ Jesus, when he (Satan) is loosed out of his prison *(Revelation Chapter 20)*; which will be the time of **another battle of Gog and Magog**.

At that time *(close of Christ Jesus reign in 1000 years)* the earthly "Gog" of Ezekiel Chapter 38 shall have been dead many, many years, and will only show up again to be judged after the second resurrection of the dead *(Revelation 20:11 through 20:14)*.

We understand from the scriptures that the first resurrection shall commence when the Church is taken out of the earth *(the rapture)*. But *Revelation 20* is the time of the second resurrection *(the resurrection of the lost dead)*. The evidence is that Satan is loosed after a thousand years. So the question also arises whether Gog and Magog of *Revelation 20:8* is the same Gog and Magog in Ezekiel Chapter 38, brought back in the second resurrection, or resurrection of the *lost dead* to face the great white throne judgment *(Revelation 20:11)*, or is this a new harvest of *(an army & mindset)* Gog and Magog allied with Satan.

Another explanation to consider is whether the scripture is also describing the unrepentant attitude that is present in Satan and his followers even after a thousand years.
One would think that after a thousand years of being bound Satan would be remorseful; realize that he is no match for God, submit by repenting, and beg God for mercy. Yet Satan behaves according to his same deceptive, disobedient old ways, and there are those that will swallow his deception and disobedience toward God even after Jesus reign a thousand years of peace in the truth. Let's just read *Revelation Chapter 20* to get a clearer understanding by filling in some details.

Dispensation *(7)* of Righteousness & Peace *(See "Definitions & Figures"* section*; associated timeline graphics are also provided)*
And I saw an angel come down from heaven; having the key of the bottomless pit and a great chain in his hand *(This angel is apparently mightier than Satan?)*.
And he laid hold on the dragon, that old serpent, which is the Devil, and Satan, and bound him a thousand years,
And cast him into the bottomless pit, and shut him up, and set a seal upon him, that he should deceive the nations no more, till the thousand years should be fulfilled: and after that he must be loosed a little season.
And I saw thrones, and they sat upon them, and judgment was given unto them: and *I saw* the souls of them that were beheaded for the witness of Jesus, and for the word of God, and which had not worshipped the beast, neither his image, neither had received *his* mark upon their foreheads, or in their hands; and they lived and reigned with Christ a thousand years.
But the rest of the dead lived not again until the thousand years were finished *(Does this mean the rest of the dead shall live again along side Satan and shall be part of another army\ mindset\ land of Gog and Magog according to Revelation 20:7 and 20:8?)*.

Revelation 20:1 through 20:5

This *is* **the first resurrection**. *(Those in the first resurrection are of the rapture of the Church in Revelation 6:12 through 6:17, and those reaped in Revelation 14:14 through 14:16 that did not receive the mark of the beast. And those Jews and non-Jews that confessed and gave themselves to the Lord Jesus Christ during tribulation of the great winepress of the wrath of God; which is also the time Israel the nation recognized Jesus as their Messiah. Jesus delivered these at the first battle encounter of Gog and Magog in Ezekiel 38 & 39, Revelation 16:16, Revelation 19:11 through 19:21, Zechariah 14)*
Blessed and holy *is* he that hath part in the first resurrection: on such the second death hath no power, but they shall be priests of God and of Christ, and shall reign with him a thousand years *(and the time Satan is in the bottomless pit)*.

Revelation 20:6

----------*Revelation 20:7 through 20:15 – Final Judgments:* ---------
Satan is judged and defeated the final time.
Earth and heaven flee from the presence of God. This means the current earth and heaven is destroyed (and\ or) prepare to be the new earth and heaven in Revelation 21:1?
The judgment and second death of the dead is brought to pass.

It sure appears that Satan has been given at least three opportunities to denounce his disobedience toward God (and the question arises, "can Satan even be forgiven"?). He was initially kicked out of heaven, rather than destroyed; He was defeated a second time according to Revelation 19:11 through 19:17 and bound in the bottomless pit for a thousand years; And now, here in Revelation 20:7 through 20:10 he still defied God; for the last time I might add.

And when the thousand years are expired, Satan shall be loosed out of his prison,
And shall go out to deceive the nations which are in the four quarters *(north, south, east, west)* of the earth, Gog and Magog, to gather them together to battle: the number of whom *is* as the sand of the

sea.

Revelation 20:7 and 20:8

*Just as before in Ezekiel 38 & 39, Revelation 16:16, Revelation
19:11 through 19:21, Zechariah 14);
The devil and those with him are allied against God and his
people; but the difference this time is that God is fresh out of
mercy and devoured them all with fire out of heaven. And the
devil that deceived them was cast into the lake of fire and
brimstone.*
And they went up on the breadth of the earth, and compassed the
camp of the saints about, and the beloved city: and fire came
down from God out of heaven, and devoured them. *(This is the
battle of Gog and Magog when God put down all rebellion to
His rule forever and ever)*
And the devil that deceived them was cast into the lake of fire and
brimstone, where the beast and the false prophet are, and shall be
tormented day and night for ever and ever.

Revelation 20:9 and 20:10

*When the great white throne judgment takes place even heaven
and earth runs from the presence of God, and there was found no
place for them. Those that were not in the first resurrection are
judged at this time. God executes the final judgment according to
the works of those recorded in his books. This includes the book of
life. Whosoever is not found written in the book of life shall be cast
into the lake of fire. The second death has torment in the lake of
fire (Refer to Revelation 20:6 and 20:10).*
And I saw a great white throne, and him that sat on it, from whose
face the earth and the heaven fled away; and there was found no
place for them. *(This indicates that God shall bring forth a new
Universe?).*
And I saw the dead, small and great, stand before God; and the
books were opened: and another book was opened, which is the
book of life: and the dead were judged out of those things which
were written in the books, according to their works.
And the sea gave up the dead which were in it; and death and hell
delivered up the dead which were in them: and they were judged
every man according to their works. *(The work that is most*

important is our faith/ confession/ acceptance/ grabbing hold of Jesus; that he has delivered us from sin unto righteousness in his death on the cross, burial, and resurrection, and he is Lord. Men shall not go to hell (to the lake of fire, the second death) because they have sin, but because they would not/ did not come to God through Jesus Christ for forgiveness of their sin).

And death and hell were cast into the lake of fire. This is the second death.

And whosoever was not found written in the book of life was cast into the lake of fire.

Revelation 20:11 through 20:15

Now, it seems obvious that the prophecy of Ezekiel Chapter 38 & 39 is about an earlier time *(at, or very close after the first resurrection because Israel is converted to Jesus and delivered from wrath)* than that of ***Revelation 20:8*** above. These are two different events that are at least a thousand years apart *(i.e., the prophecy of Ezekiel Chapter 38 & 39 taking place just before the thousand years; and Revelation 20:8 taking place after the thousand years)*. But the spirit and purpose of Satan, "Gog and Magog" is equally present in each event to destroy the people of God.

Prophecy of the Battle of Gog and Magog:
Notice in ***Revelation 20:9*** God devoured, with fire, those *(Gog and Magog: the number of whom is as the sand of the sea)* that would destroy his people. Actually, there is no battle; God just incinerate the entire rebellious troop in a moment of time!

Prophecy of the Battle of Armageddon:
This obviously is the battle Ezekiel prophecies in his Chapters of Ezekiel 38 & 39!
And in the prophecy of Ezekiel the enemy will die, then the birds, and beasts of the field shall consume their flesh *(Ezekiel 39:4)*, but many were buried, including the ruler Gog, descendant of Magog. Next, let's just begin reading at Ezekiel Chapter 38:1, and examine, more closely, what is being revealed concerning the "Battle of Armageddon", lead by the chief earthly prince Gog.

Ezekiel's Prophecy of the Battle of Armageddon Includes Satan!
And the word of the LORD came unto me, saying,
Son of man, set thy face against Gog, the land of Magog, the chief
    prince of Meshech and Tubal, and prophesy against him,
And say, Thus saith the Lord GOD; Behold, I *am* against thee, O
    Gog, the chief prince of Meshech and Tubal:
***These are descendants of Japheth, which we read about in Genesis
Chapter 10. This people have migrated (during the centuries) to
those parts of the earth north of Israel. As we continue reading we
will see that they came out of the "north parts" against Israel, to
destroy them, as Gog and Magog.***
Ezekiel 38:1 through 38:3

And I will turn thee back, and put hooks into thy jaws, and I will
    bring thee forth, and all thine army, horses and horsemen, all of
    them clothed with all sorts *of armour, even* a great company *with*
    bucklers and shields, all of them handling swords:
Persia ***(present day Iran and surrounding nations)***, Ethiopia, and
    Libya with them; all of them with shield and helmet: ***(Biblical
    Persia included much more territory than present day Iran)***
Gomer, and all his bands; the house of Togarmah of the north
    quarters, and all his bands: *and* many people with thee.
Be thou prepared ***(Gog)***, and prepare for thyself, thou, and all thy
    company that are assembled unto thee, and be thou a guard unto
    them.
After many days thou shalt be visited: in the latter years thou shalt
    come into the land ***(Israel)*** *that is* brought back from the sword,
    and is gathered out of many people ***(or nations?)***, against the
    mountains of Israel, which have been always waste: but it
    (Israel) is brought forth out of the nations ***(where they have been
    scattered)***, and they shall dwell safely all of them ***(the remnant,
    Judah of Israel)***.
Ezekiel 38:4 through 38:8

The reference to ***"the latter years" in Ezekiel 38:8*** above imply that
this will be a time just before, or at the very return of Christ Jesus;
when God will have turned his primary focus to Israel once again
(i.e., the rapture at the time of Revelation 6:12 may have already

occurred).

From the time of Christ unto now, the Church has been the number one earthly concern in the kingdom of God. But when the Church has been taken out of the earth, Israel shall become the first priority on earth again. In other words God will have accomplished the task of grafting gentile into his family, then he will turns His total attention to Israel again.

The first shall have become last, and the last shall be first.

This will be the time when the enemies of Israel will be determined to totally destroy her like never before.

And so, I am persuaded from the time of Revelation 6:12 unto the time of the final words of Revelation 19:21, Daniel's final ½ week, or 3 ½ years will have been fulfilled; Israel's enemies defeated; and Dispensation (7) of Righteousness & Peace (or the 1000 years prepared to start)! (See the paragraph, "Dispensations" in the "Definitions & Figures" section; associated timeline graphics are also provided).

Thou *(Gog, and Satan)* shalt ascend and come like a storm, thou shalt be like a cloud *(for the multitude)* to cover the land, thou, and all thy bands, and many people with thee.

Thus saith the Lord GOD; It shall also come to pass, *that* at the same time shall things come into thy *(Gog's)* mind, and thou shalt think an evil thought:

And thou shalt say, I will go up to the land of unwalled villages; I will go to them that are at rest, that dwell safely, all of them dwelling without walls, and having neither bars nor gates,

(This brings to mind the terrorists that come against the democratic nations of the earth, including Israel).

To take a spoil, and to take a prey; to turn thine hand upon the desolate places *that are now* inhabited, and upon the people *(Judah of Israel)* *that are* gathered out of the nations, which have gotten cattle and goods, that dwell in the midst of the land.

Sheba, and Dedan, and the merchants of Tarshish, with all the young lions thereof, shall say unto thee *(Gog)*, Art thou come to take a spoil? hast thou gathered thy company to take a prey? to carry away silver and gold, to take away cattle and goods, to take a great spoil?

Therefore, son of man, prophesy and say unto Gog, Thus saith the

Lord GOD; In that day when my people of Israel dwelleth safely, shalt thou not know *it*?

And thou shalt come from thy place out of the north parts, thou, and many people with thee, all of them riding upon horses, a great company, and a mighty army:

And thou shalt come up against my people of Israel, as a cloud *(for the multitude)* to cover the land; it shall be in the latter days *(or end times)*, and I will bring thee against my land, that the heathen may know me, when I shall be sanctified in thee, O Gog, before their eyes.

Thus saith the Lord GOD; *Art* thou he of whom I have spoken in old time by my servants the prophets of Israel, which prophesied in those days *many* years that I would bring thee against them *(my people Israel)*?

Ezekiel 38:9 through 38:17

A search of the scriptures was conducted, and it was determined that the name "Gog" appears in *1ˢᵗ Chronicles 5:4, Ezekiel 38 and 39, and Revelation 20:8*. But, *Ezekiel 38 verse 17* above says, "Art thou he of whom I have spoken in old time by my servants the prophet(s) of Israel, which prophesied in those days many years ...". So the question arises, what is *verse 17* talking about? Where is the prophecy concerning Gog many years before now?

The answer is, *verse 17* is written directly to the fallen angel "Satan" who is influencing Gog, of the land of Magog, to come against Israel.

From the time the Lord GOD brought forth this new creature man in the garden, Satan was there with evil influence.

There are many scriptures throughout the Bible that prophecy against Satan, but Gog is only referenced in *1ˢᵗ Chronicles 5:4, Ezekiel 38 & 39, and Revelation 20:8.*

And it shall come to pass at the same time when Gog shall come against the land of Israel, saith the Lord GOD, *that* my fury shall come up in my face.

For in my jealousy *and* in the fire of my wrath have I spoken, Surely in that day *(of a mighty earthquake; Revelation 6:12 rapture of the Church must take place before the wrath of God; the day of the LORD; Zechariah Chapter 14?)* there shall be a great shaking in the land of Israel;

So that the fishes of the sea, and the fowls of the heaven, and the beasts of the field, and all creeping things that creep upon the earth, and all the men that *are* upon the face of the earth, shall shake at my presence, and the mountains shall be thrown down, and the steep places shall fall, and every wall shall fall to the ground.

And I will call for a sword against him *(Gog of Magog, and Satan)* throughout all my mountains, saith the Lord GOD: every man's sword shall be against his brother *(kind of sound like the world at war, doesn't it?)*.

And I will plead against him *(Gog)* with pestilence and with blood; and I will rain upon him, and upon his bands, and upon the many people that *are* with him, an overflowing rain, and great hailstones, fire, and brimstone.

Thus will I magnify myself, and sanctify myself; and I will be known in the eyes of many nations, and they shall know that I *am* the LORD.

Ezekiel 38:18 through 38:23

The prophecy of the Battle of Armageddon continues …
This prophecy continues through the end of *Ezekiel Chapter 39*. So, let's just continue reading.

Therefore, thou son of man, prophesy against Gog, and say, Thus saith the Lord GOD; Behold, I *am* against thee, O Gog, the chief prince of Meshech and Tubal:

And I will turn thee back, and leave but the sixth part of thee *(one out of six)*, and will cause thee to come up from the north parts, and will bring thee upon the mountains of Israel:

And I will smite thy bow out of thy left hand, and will cause thine arrows to fall out of thy right hand *(the ability of Gog to make war is taken away)*.

Thou shalt fall upon the mountains of Israel, thou, and all thy bands, and the people that *is* with thee: I will give thee unto the ravenous birds of every sort, and *to* the beasts of the field to be devoured.

Thou shalt fall upon the open field: for I have spoken *it*, saith the Lord GOD.

And I will send a fire on Magog, and among them that dwell
carelessly *(or unconcerned?)* in the isles: and they shall know
that I am the LORD.
So will I make my holy name known in the midst of my people
Israel; and I will not let them pollute my holy name any more:
and the heathen shall know that I am the LORD, the Holy One in
Israel.

Ezekiel 39:1 through 39:7

Although many individuals of Judah of Israel have seen, and
accepted Jesus as their Messiah these past centuries, the Nation
State, ***"Judah of Israel"*** has not. But at this time in Ezekiel's
prophesy they will see, and not be allowed to pollute the name of the
Holy One in Israel any more, as talked about in ***Ezekiel Chapter
39:7*** above. Later, at the end of this prophesy, we read in ***Ezekiel
39:29*** where the Lord GOD declares, ***"Neither will I hide my face
any more from them"***. Let's just continue reading until we get to this
scripture.

Behold, it is come, and it is done, saith the Lord GOD; this is the day
whereof I have spoken.
And they that dwell in the cities of Israel shall go forth, and shall set
on fire and burn the weapons, both the shields and the bucklers,
the bows and the arrows, and the handstaves, and the spears, and
they shall burn them with fire seven *(7)* years:
So that they shall take no wood out of the field, neither cut down any
out of the forests; for they shall burn the weapons with fire: and
they shall spoil those that spoiled them, and rob those that robbed
them, saith the Lord GOD.

Ezekiel 39:8 through 39:10

And it shall come to pass in that day, that I will give unto Gog a
place *(memorial?)* there of graves in Israel, the valley of the
passengers *(passer-by; sightseer?)* on the east of the sea
(Mediterranean?): and it shall stop the noses of the passengers:
and there shall they bury Gog and all his multitude: and they
shall call it The valley of Hamongog. *(A place the sightseer
would visit; in other words a memorial park of graves to
advertise the awesome power of God; entire valley of nothing*

except grave markers?)

And seven *(7)* months shall the house of Israel be burying of them, that they may cleanse the land.

Yea, all the people of the land shall bury *them*; and it shall be to them a renown the day that I *(Jesus)* shall be glorified, saith the Lord GOD.

And they shall sever *(hire)* out men of continual employment, passing through the land to bury with the passengers those that remain upon the face of the earth, to cleanse it: after the end of seven *(7)* months shall they search.

And the passengers *that* pass through the land, when *any* seeth a man's bone, then shall he set up a sign by it, till the buriers have buried it in the valley of Hamongog.

And also the name of the city *(of the valley of Hamongog)* *shall be* Hamonah. Thus shall they cleanse the land.

Jesus also prophesied of these next five (5) verses in Matthew 24:27 through 24:31; and Luke 17:24 through 17:31

And, thou son of man, thus saith the Lord GOD; Speak unto every feathered fowl, and to every beast of the field, Assemble yourselves, and come; gather yourselves on every side to my sacrifice that I do sacrifice for you, *even* a great sacrifice upon the mountains of Israel, that ye may eat flesh, and drink blood.

Ye shall eat the flesh of the mighty, and drink the blood of the princes of the earth, of rams, of lambs, and of goats, of bullocks, all of them fatlings of Bashan.

And ye shall eat fat till ye be full, and drink blood till ye be drunken, of my sacrifice which I have sacrificed for you.

Thus ye shall be filled at my table with horses and chariots, with mighty men, and with all men of war, saith the Lord GOD.

And I will set my glory among the heathen, and all the heathen shall see my judgment that I have executed, and my hand that I have laid upon them.

National Israel is Saved and Delivered When They Finally See and Accept Jesus; Messiah

So the house of Israel shall know that I *am* the LORD their God from that day and forward *(Israel reconstituted a Nation State again since 1948 A.D.; National Israel shall finally see that Jesus is Messiah; the Son of their Fathers God)*.

And the heathen shall know that the house of Israel went into captivity for their iniquity: because they trespassed against me, therefore hid I my face from them, and gave them into the hand of their enemies: so fell they all by the sword.

According to their uncleanness and according to their transgressions have I done unto them, and hid my face from them.

Therefore thus saith the Lord GOD; Now will I bring again the captivity *(or obedience)* of Jacob, and have mercy upon the whole house of Israel, and will be jealous for my holy name;

After that they have borne their shame, and all their trespasses whereby they have trespassed against me, when they dwelt safely in their land, and none made *them* afraid.

When I have brought them again from the *(other)* people *(on the Planet)*, and gathered them out of their enemies' lands, and am sanctified in them in the sight of many nations;

Then shall they know that I *am* the LORD their God, which caused them to be led into captivity among the heathen: but I have gathered them unto their own land, and have left none of them any more there.

Neither will I hide my face any more from them: for I have poured out my spirit *(the Holy Spirit)* upon the house of Israel, saith the Lord GOD.

Ezekiel 39:11 through 39:29

When shall these things commence to occur?

The occurrence of events in this prophecy can be discussed in terms of the timeline of Daniels "seventy weeks".

While in captivity for nearly 70 years after the Babylonian invasion of Judah of Israel, Daniel sought answers from God based on Jeremiah's prophecy *(Jeremiah 25:11 thru 12, Jeremiah 29:10)* that his people would remain in captivity for seventy *(70)* years. In Jeremiah's prophecy God also promised that he would return Judah to their land after the seventy years.

Well, Daniel realizes that the seventy years is close at hand, or has already passed. So we see Daniel consulting God through prayer about this in *Daniel Chapter 9*. Take a moment to read *verses 1 through 23 of Daniel Chapter 9* from your Bible, and our paragraph with the title, *"When Does Daniel's Prophecy of Seventy Weeks Begin & End"*, which is provided in the *"Definitions & Figures" section.* Then let's continue our analysis together at *Daniel 9:24* below.

Daniel Chapter 9 verse 24 …

Seventy weeks are determined upon thy people and upon thy holy city, to finish the transgression, and to make an end of sins, and to make reconciliation for iniquity, and to bring in everlasting righteousness, and to seal up the vision and prophecy, and to anoint the most Holy.

Know therefore and understand, *that* from the going forth of the commandment to restore and to build Jerusalem unto the Messiah the Prince *shall be* seven weeks, and threescore and two weeks *(69 weeks or 483 years)*: the street shall be built again, and the wall, even in troublous times.

And after threescore and two weeks *(62 weeks, or 434 years; i.e., rebuilding efforts have ceased on the city wall)* shall Messiah be cut off, but not for himself: and the people of the prince that shall come shall destroy the city and the sanctuary; and the end thereof *shall be* with a flood, and unto the end of the war desolations are determined *(This is referring to the seventy (70) A.D. destruction of Jerusalem by the Romans!)*.

And he *(Messiah)* shall confirm the covenant with many for one week: and in the midst of the week he *(Messiah)* shall cause the *(animal)* sacrifice and the oblation to cease *(which is Dispensation (5) of Law being set aside, also, when Messiah Jesus fulfills it by His sacrifice)*, and for the overspreading of abominations he shall make *it (animal sacrifice)* desolate, even until the consummation *(when Jesus appears the second time)*, and that determined *(the sacrifice of Jesus establishing Dispensation (6) of Grace and Mercy)* shall be poured upon *(or put in place of)* the desolate *(animal sacrifice, and\ or Dispensation (5))*.

Daniel 9:24 through 9:27

Daniel 9, verse 24 says there is a time period remaining in which God will work out promises and prophecy that were made to Israel, then he will bring in everlasting righteousness. During this time period, *(which is now known to be seventy weeks of years; one week representing seven years, for a total of 490 years)*, the following things shall be accomplished:

    a. There will be an end of transgression - Mercy is now available through Jesus Christ for forgiveness of sin. God accepts the sacrifice of Jesus as paying the sin debt for anyone that will come to Him confessing Jesus as savior.

    b. There will be an end of sin - Jesus died for the sins of man, but the time of God's judgment will end sin whether everyone has accepted Jesus or not.

    c. Reconciliation for iniquity will be made - Men will be reconciled unto God; no longer counted as an enemy of God.

    d. The most holy will be anointed - This happened in *John 1:29 through 1:32*. God the Father anointed Jesus with the *Holy Spirit and His Power. This is not talking about a "brick, mortar, wood, etc ..." man made temple structure. The Tabernacle of Moses; the Temple Solomon built; the rebuilt Temple dedicated by Zerubbabel after the Babylonian destruction; and the Temple during the Roman Empire Era (with their animal sacrifices) were figure & types of Messiah Jesus; the "Living Eternal Temple and Sacrifice"! There is no purpose now in our "Dispensation (6) of Grace" for those "representative practices" that were of "Dispensation (5) of Law; Don't You See? We have a direct line to God in Christ Jesus; and in fact He (Jesus) is God manifest in human flesh! It is He that is the "most holy".*

       e. The vision and prophecy will be fulfilled - This particular vision and prophesy, "the 70 weeks", will be fulfilled. And all the promises God has made by his prophets and *Word/ Jesus* will come to pass.

       f. Everlasting righteousness will be established - The Kingdom of God will prevail on earth.

It becomes obvious that *1-week represents 7 years* when we apply years to the explanations given in scripture; *Daniel Chapter 9, verses 25 and 26*. Events that have occurred surrounding the rebuilding of the Temple; the City, and City wall coincide with Daniel's prophecies. And according to the years Daniel prophesied, the Messiah *(Jesus)* came to the Jews; ministered for 3 ½ years, and was cut off *(or crucified)*.

The city and sanctuary was destroyed again after Jesus resurrection. This last time the destruction was by the *Romans in 70 A.D*. Jesus told the people that this would happen in *Luke 19:41 through 19:44, Matt. 24:1 and 24:2; & Mark 13:1 and 13:2*. The Temple has not been rebuilt, even until this present time *(2022 A.D)*. The Temple Mount and Israel is desolate in that a none-Jewish worship place has been there for centuries. The Jewish people are left with having to pray at the "Western Wall", which is the only remaining part of the Temple structure King Herod the Great refurbished that once stood on the Temple Mount. They are in desolation because they have no way of accessing God *(i.e. there is no temple; they rejected Jesus according to Luke 19:41 through 19:44; they were scattered throughout the nations of the world after 70 A.D.)*.

Daniel Chapter 9, verse 25 and 26 explained
Daniel Chapter 9, verses 25 and 26 are saying, begin counting *(in years)* when the command go forth to rebuild Jerusalem, and count *483 years (or 69 weeks)* into the future. After that is when the Messiah shall come, *"the first time"*. Then, when the city wall is completed *(i.e., efforts on the City wall ceases)* begin counting again, and count *434 years (or 62 weeks)* into the future. After that is when Messiah shall be cut off *(in the middle of the week, which we know now was 3 ½ -years into the 7 year (or 1-week) ministering Jesus was suppose to confirm with the Jewish people)*.

Now, *"the people of the prince that shall come"* is Rome's military general and soldiers that destroyed the city in *70 A.D.* The desolations determined are that the Jewish people have no sanctuary for worship, and they were scattered throughout the nations of the world until *1948 A.D.* At that time God began gathering them into their homeland *(Israel)* again. The generation that witnesses this *(Israel's restoration)* shall not pass away until all be accomplished according to prophecy?

Daniel Chapter 9, verse 27 explained
And he *(Messiah, not the prince of the people that shall come, nor the man of sin)* shall confirm the covenant with many for *one week, or 7 years*: and in the midst of the week he shall cause the *(animal)* sacrifice and oblation to cease. No one can cause what God has established to be desolate, except God. It can be misused, abused; maybe even delayed; but not change the purpose God intended, nor removed.
When Jesus was crucified he was sacrificed one time for all sin. The Jewish system of *animal sacrifice* is made obsolete and\ or desolate *(and for the overspreading of abominations he shall make it desolate).*

I am persuaded it is abomination leading to blasphemy to reject; ignore; discount; treat with discuss anything the LORD God gives, or does for the cause of delivering the human race from its terminal state of sin and death! We must remember in the eyes of God we were born in this terminal state since Adam sinned; and we must be born again, or born the second (2nd) time. How do we know this? Because it is obvious death is 100%, and the Word of God says so!
But it may be that God considers "knowledge" before holding one guilty of such an offense against Him (God our Creator); which is blasphemy of the Holy Spirit. And the standards of knowledge the LORD God applies may not, or hardly ever, be as we think!
But we can be confident that Antiochus IV of Epiphanies committed a blasphemous act of abomination and desolation, when he sacrificed a pig to the Greek god Zeus, on the Altar at Jerusalem, as recorded by secular history! Daniel Chapter 11:31

prophesied this would occur; and so it did about the year 167 B.C.; many years after Daniel.
Antiochus' action violated; rejected; treated with discuss, efforts of God our Creator to rescue individuals from the terminal state of sin and death!
The switch for powering eternity can not be turned on until all is in place; no matter how many so called, "gods" may try to activate it! And the final place that must be filled is; you got it, God the Creator! Therefore, not even the "man of sin backed by Satan" is able to delete what God put in place and wills.

But today in Dispensation *(6)* of Grace animal sacrifice is no longer acceptable to God to atone for sin; it has fulfilled its purpose and is desolate *(even until the consummation, which is the second (2nd) coming of Jesus)*.
There is a pre-scheduled time when Jesus will consummate the covenant with his follows. The desolation of Israel *(i.e., not having a place to worship\ access to God)* will continue even unto that time *(and that determined; the sacrifice of Jesus shall be poured upon (or put in place of) the desolate animal sacrifice)*. And what Jesus has done in his sacrifice, fulfills, or is put in place of that which is now desolate *(the animal sacrifice)*. The sacrifice of Jesus has superseded the purpose for daily animal sacrifice as handed down by Moses in the Old Testament *(See Deuteronomy 18:15 through 18:22; Moses said to "hear Him")*!

For a period of *1-week (7 years)* Jesus was suppose to confirm God's promises to the Jews according to the Old Testament. But the *religious National ruling authority* rejected him and he was crucified just *3 1/2-years (or 1/2-week)* after His Ministry began. His death, as far as God is concerned, caused the daily *animal* sacrifice to cease. Animal sacrifice no longer has any benefit for those that would practice it.

And so, the *time clock of Daniels 70 weeks* is also suspended at the resurrection of Jesus because the *National Jewish Authority of Israel* rejected him according to *Luke 19:41 through 19:44*.
In case no one has noticed, God has removed the Jew's capacity to practice animal sacrifice. No Jewish person of authority is even

allowed to visit the ***Temple Mount in Jerusalem***. During the time of Jesus return, that ***final 1/2-week (or 3 1/2-years)*** will be continued and fulfilled ***(this is also referred to as the time of Jacob's trouble, or Jacob's woes)***. It is at that time the ***seventy weeks, or 490 years*** of Daniel's prophecy will be completed with the Jewish people. **This will also be the time of the prophecy of Ezekiel Chapter 38 and 39, which Revelation 16:16 calls the Battle of Armageddon.**

Understand that the ***"Church Age"*** is not counted as part of the ***70-weeks or 490 years, and that the count of Daniel's 70th week ceased at 69 ½ weeks, or 486 ½ years (i.e., when Jesus was crucified)***. Also, keep in mind the prayers of Daniel were for his people, the Nation of Israel. ***When Jesus talked about the last days, he was referring to the 70th week, and final 3 1/2-years of Daniel's 70 (seventy) -weeks; which have been (2022 A.D. – 34 A.D. = 1988 years) thus far to-date, because the years of the Church Age are not included with Daniel's 70 –weeks (or 490 years). Is there anything too hard for the LORD?***

End Time Men and Their Authorities

Authority of Kingdoms Ruled by Men is Taken Away

Perhaps you have wondered if there is a relationship between Gog of Magog and the man of sin. For example, are they the same individual; if they are not the same individual, then where does their exploits occur relative to each other on the timeline of human history?

But make no mistake, these individuals and many others besides them are antichrist:

1Jn 4:3 And every spirit that confesseth not that Jesus Christ is come in the flesh is not of God: and this is that *spirit* of antichrist, whereof ye have heard that it should come; and even now already is it in the world.

Our study traces prophecies and revealed events that shall culminate in the two greatest battles that shall ever be known of human kind; the ***Battle of Armageddon***, led by the ruler Gog, descendant of Magog, as described in ***Ezekiel Chapters 38 & 39*** at the return of Jesus, and the ***Battle of Gog and Magog as described in Revelation 20:7 through 20:10*** at the time Satan shall be cast into the lake that burns with fire and brimstone.

The final texts of our study consists of Bible Scriptures that have been singled out as pertaining to the times and events of these great battles. Some Scriptures are chosen because it seems they shall contribute to, or occur around the same time as the battle event(s). We will examine these particular Scriptures in an effort to determine the relationship, if any, between the ruler Gog of Magog and the man of sin *(the beast of Revelation Chapters 12 & 13, and Daniel Chapter 7)*; and when these battles shall occur on the timeline of human history.

The Seventh of the Seven Trumpets Mark the End of Kingdoms Ruled by Men

And the seventh angel sounded; and there were great voices in heaven, saying, The kingdoms of this world are become *the kingdoms* of our Lord, and of his Christ; and he shall reign for ever and ever.

And the four and twenty *(24)* elders, which sat before God on their
seats, fell upon their faces, and worshipped God,

Saying, We give thee thanks, O Lord God Almighty, which art, and
wast, and art to come; because thou hast taken to thee thy great
power, and hast reigned.

And the nations were angry, and thy wrath is come, and the time of
the dead, that they should be judged, and that thou shouldest give
reward unto thy servants the prophets, and to the saints, and them
that fear thy name, small and great; and shouldest destroy them
which destroy the earth.

***The wrath of God; more environmental disasters and earthquakes
are unleashed on earth.***

And the temple of God was opened in heaven, and there was seen in
his temple the ark of his testament ***(his word, the Lord Jesus
Christ which is the ark of covenant between God and man)***: and
there were lightnings, and voices, and thunderings, and an
earthquake, and great hail.

Revelation 11:15 through 11:19

**The Time of the End of Kingdoms Ruled by Men as Described in
"a, b, c, d" that follows:**

a. And he *(the man of sin)* shall speak *great* words against the most
High, and shall wear out the saints of the most High, and think to
change times and laws: and they *(the saints)* shall be given into
his hand **until a time and times and the dividing of time.**

Daniel 7:25

b. And I heard the man clothed in linen, which *was* upon the waters
of the river, when he held up his right hand and his left hand unto
heaven, and sware by him that liveth for ever that ***it (time of
kingdoms ruled by men) shall be* for a time, times, and an
half; and when he *(God)* shall have accomplished to scatter
the power of the holy people, all these *things* shall be finished
*(or when God is done revealing who he is, all these things shall
be finished).***

Daniel 12:7

c. And to the woman *(Israel)* were given two wings of a great
eagle, that she might fly into the wilderness, into her place,

33

where she is nourished *(sustained/ kept alive)* **for a time, and times, and half a time**, from the face of the serpent *(the devil)*.

d. And the woman fled into the wilderness, where she hath a place prepared of God, that they should feed her there *(or have the Gospel of Jesus preached to her)* **a thousand two hundred** *and* **threescore** *(1260)* **days** *(3.452 years)*.

Revelation 12:14 & 12:6

The Time of the Battle of Armageddon, Whose Leader is Ezekiel's Gog of Magog

And the sixth *(6th)* angel poured out his vial *(the sixth of the seven last plagues of God; the great winepress)* upon the great river Euphrates; and the water thereof was dried up, that the way of the kings of the east might be prepared.

And I saw three unclean spirits like frogs *(one unclean spirit came)* out of the mouth of the dragon *(Satan the devil)*, and *(one unclean spirit came)* out of the mouth of the beast *(man of sin, earthly world ruling individual)*, and *(one unclean spirit came)* out of the mouth of the false prophet *(false holy man?)*.

For they are the spirits of devils, working miracles, *which* go forth unto the kings of the earth and of the whole world, to gather them to the battle of that great day of God Almighty.

Behold, I *(Jesus, Son of God)* come as a thief. Blessed *is* he that watcheth, and keepeth his garments, lest he walk naked, and they see his shame.

And he *(Son of God)* gathered them together into a place called in the Hebrew tongue Armageddon. *(This is the first encounter of Gog and Magog, which is also the prophecy of Ezekiel Chapters 38 and 39. But there is another Gog and Magog prophesied in Revelation 20:7 through 20:11; occurring after the thousand (1000) years of Righteousness & Peace; Dispensation (7)).*

Revelation 16:12 through 16:16

The Seventh of Seven Vials of the Last Plagues; The Great Winepress of the Wrath of God is poured out upon the Earth

And the seventh *(7th)* angel poured out his vial into the air; and there came a great voice out of the temple of heaven, from the throne, saying, It *(the tribulation of God upon earth)* is done.

34

Revelation Chapters 17 and 18 describes the final impact upon "the world, Babylon, the great whore" resulting from the tribulations God poured out upon the earth.

Revelation 16:17

The fate of the Ruler, Gog of Magog (Ezekiel's Gog, Part 1)

Behold, it is come, and it is done, saith the Lord GOD; this *is* the day whereof I have spoken.

And they that dwell in the cities of Israel shall go forth, and shall set on fire and burn the weapons, both the shields and the bucklers, the bows and the arrows, and the handstaves, and the spears, and they shall burn them with fire seven *(7)* years:

So that they shall take no wood out of the field, neither cut down *any* out of the forests; for they shall burn the weapons with fire: and they shall spoil those that spoiled them, and rob those that robbed them, saith the Lord GOD.

And it shall come to pass in that day, *that* I will give unto Gog a place there of graves in Israel, the valley of the passengers on the east of the sea *(Mediterranean)*: and it shall stop the *noses* of the passengers: and there shall they bury Gog and all his multitude: and they shall call *it* The valley of Hamongog.

Ezekiel 39:8 through 39:11

The fate of the Beast; World ruling Power, the Man of Sin (Part 1)

And I saw the beast, and the kings of the earth, and their armies, gathered together to make war against him *(Jesus, King of kings)* that sat on the horse, and against his army *(saints, and angel of heaven)*.

And the beast was taken, and with him the false prophet that wrought miracles before him *(the beast)*, with which he deceived them that had received the mark of the beast, and them that worshipped his image. These both were cast alive into a lake of fire burning with brimstone *(in others words these individuals were not permitted to die the first death; but God sent them directly to the second death, which is a lake of fire burning with brimstone!)*.

Revelation 19:19 and 19:20

The Time of the Battle of Revelation's Gog and Magog

And when the thousand years *(Dispensation (7) of Righteousness &*
Peace) are expired, Satan shall be loosed out of his prison,
And shall go out to deceive the nations which are in the four quarters
of the earth, Gog and Magog, to gather them together to battle:
the number of whom *is* as the sand of the sea.
And they went up on the breadth of the earth, and compassed the
camp of the saints about, and the beloved city *(Jerusalem)*: and
fire came down from God out of heaven, and devoured them.
*(This is the Battle of Gog and Magog when God put down all
rebellion against Him, and He shall rule forever and ever)*
And the devil that deceived them was cast into the lake of fire and
brimstone *(second death)*, where the beast and the false prophet
are, and shall be tormented day and night for ever and ever.
And I saw a great white throne, and him that sat on it, from whose
face the earth and the heaven fled away; and there was found no
place for them. *(This indicates that God shall bring forth a new,
and/or reconditioned Universe).*

Revelation 20:7 through 20:11

The Man of Sin Violated "Kingdoms Ruled by Men That Was Taken Away"

And the seventh angel sounded *(his Trumpet)*; and there were great voices in heaven, saying, The kingdoms of this world are become *the kingdoms* of our Lord, and of his Christ; and he shall reign for ever and ever.

And the four and twenty *(24)* elders, which sat before God on their seats, fell upon their faces, and worshipped God,

Saying, We give thee thanks, O Lord God Almighty, which art, and wast, and art to come; because thou hast taken to thee thy great power, and hast reigned.

And the nations were angry, and thy wrath is come, and the time of the dead, that they should be judged, and that thou shouldest give reward unto thy servants the prophets, and to the saints, and them that fear *(honor\ respect)* thy name, small and great; and shouldest destroy them which destroy the earth.

The wrath of God; more environmental disasters and earthquakes are unleashed on earth.

And the temple of God was opened in heaven, and there was seen in his temple the ark of his testament *(his word, the Lord Jesus Christ which is the ark of covenant between man and God)*: and there were lightnings, and voices, and thunderings, and an earthquake, and great hail.

Revelation 11:15 through 11:19

These scriptures (Revelation 11:15 through 11:19) also describe the conditions that will exist at the time the Lord God shall rescind the "Authority of men to rule." At this time, and forward, all governing authority of man on earth shall be in defiance of God. It shall be the time when the seventh of the seven angels sounds his trumpet during the tribulation period of God, and it is before the man of sin shall have gain world rule. Therefore, the reign of the man of sin (Revelation Chapter 12 and 13) shall be in defiance of God before it started, and from the very beginning.

A Time of Calm and Presumed Hope; Revelation 12 through Revelation 14:20:

The times and events of Revelation 12:1 through Revelation 14:20 associated with the reign of the man of sin; the beast, are between the end of the seven (7) trumpet judgments (Revelation 11:19), and the beginning of the seven (7) last plagues (or great winepress of the wrath of God) beginning at Revelation 16:1. This will be a short time of calm and presumed hope, whereby the man of sin will claim credit for bringing to pass.

At some point during this time the man of sin will declare himself God; "presumably from the newly constructed Jewish Temple" on Jerusalem's Temple Mount (Revelation 11:1 through 11:13). But notice, there are no physical measurements given for the new Temple; and it is given unto the Gentiles to occupy the area of the court while they tread the holy city under foot forty and two months (or 1260 days). Therefore, could it be the "man of sin" shall declare his "God" status from whatever brick, mortar, and wood man made temple that is on the Temple Mount at the time? It may be this restarts the count of Daniel's final 1/2 week, or 3 ½ years (i.e., forty and two months)?

Keep in mind the <u>reality</u> that Jesus in Jerusalem is the living Temple and resurrected Sacrifice in Jerusalem! And so, this may very well be the appointed season & time of the return of Christ Jesus as described in Revelation 19:11 through 19:21, Ezekiel Chapters 38 & 39, Zechariah Chapter 14, and as prophesied by Daniel in the scriptures below:

And from the time *that* the daily *(animal)* sacrifice shall be taken away, and the abomination that maketh desolate set up *(the man of sin declaring himself God)*, *there shall be* a thousand two hundred and ninety *(1290)* days *(3.534 years)*.

Blessed *is* he *(Jesus at His second (2nd) coming)* that waiteth, and cometh to the thousand three hundred and five and thirty *(1335)* days *(3.657 years; or 45 days after the 1290 days; i.e., the final ½ week, or 3 ½ years of Daniel's 70 weeks resumes count again and continues to fulfilling the prophecy! Then Dispensation (7) of Righteousness & Peace (the 1000 years) begins shortly after)*.

Daniel 12:11 through 12:12

Daniel's Prophecy of the "Times" of the End of Kingdoms Ruled by Men as given in "e, f, g, h" below:

I *(Daniel)* saw in the night visions, and, behold, one like the Son of man came with the clouds of heaven, and came to the Ancient of days, and they *(angels in Daniel's vision)* brought him *(Son of man; Jesus)* near before him *(Ancient of days)*.

And there was given him *(Son of man; Jesus)* dominion, and glory, and a kingdom, that all people, nations, and languages, should serve him: his *(Son of man; Jesus)* dominion is an everlasting dominion, which shall not pass away, and his *(Son of man; Jesus)* kingdom that which shall not be destroyed.

I Daniel was grieved in my spirit in the midst of my body, and the visions of my head troubled me.

I came near unto one of them *(angel in Daniel's vision)* that stood by, and asked him the truth of all this. So he told me, and made me know the interpretation of the things.

These great beasts, which are four *(4)*, are four *(4)* kings *(world ruling powers)*, which shall arise out of the earth *(during their time in history)*.

But the saints of the most High *(God)* shall take the kingdom, and possess the kingdom *(world ruling power)* for ever, even for ever and ever.

Then I would know the truth of the fourth *(4th)* beast *(world ruling power that began as the Roman Empire)*, which was diverse from all the others, exceeding dreadful, whose teeth were of iron, and his nails of brass; which devoured, brake in pieces, and stamped the residue with his feet;

And of the ten *(10)* horns *(or nations)* that were in his head, and of the other *(single horn/ nation)* which came up, and before whom three *(of the ten horns/ nations)* fell; even of that horn that had eyes, and a mouth that spake very great things, whose look was more stout than his fellows *(ten horns/ nations)*.

I beheld, and the same horn made war with the saints, and prevailed against them;

Until *(a time and times and the dividing of time)* the Ancient of days came, and judgment was given to the saints of the most High; and the time came that the saints possessed the kingdom *(world ruling power)*.

Thus he said, The fourth *(4ᵗʰ)* beast shall be the fourth *(4ᵗʰ)* kingdom
(world ruling power) upon earth, which shall be diverse from all
kingdoms, and shall devour the whole earth, and shall tread it
down, and break it in pieces.

And the ten *(10)* horns out of this kingdom *(world ruling power)* are
ten *(10)* kings that shall arise: and another *(single horn)* shall
rise after them; and he shall be diverse from the first, and he shall
subdue three kings *(of the ten)*.

The first, "time and times"

e   And he *(single horn that subdue three of the ten)* shall speak
great words against the most High *(God)*, and shall wear out the
saints of the most High, and think to change times and laws: and
they *(the saints)* shall be given into his hand **until a time and
times and the dividing of time** *(which shall be the days of the
second (2ⁿᵈ) coming of the Lord Jesus Christ)*.

Daniel 7:13 through 7:25

And he *(man of sin, enemy of Israel)* shall plant the tabernacles of
his palace between the seas in the glorious holy mountain
(Jerusalem); yet he shall come to his end, and none shall help
him *(Can this be the Islamic Temple that is on the Temple
Mount since about 700 to 650 A.D.?)*.

And at that time shall Michael stand up, the great prince which
standeth for the children of thy people: and there shall be a time
of trouble, such as never was since there was a nation even to
that same time: and at that time thy people *(Judah of Israel)*
shall be delivered, every one that shall be found written in the
book.

And many of them that sleep in the dust of the earth shall awake,
some to everlasting life, and some to shame and everlasting
contempt *(The rapture occurring first; Revelation's
Tribulation, then the Great White Throne judgment after the
thousand years of Righteousness & Peace (Dispensation (7))*.

And they that be wise shall shine as the brightness of the firmament;
and they that turn many to righteousness as the stars for ever and
ever.

But thou, O Daniel, shut up the words, and seal the book, even to the
time of the end: many shall run to and fro, and knowledge shall
be increased.

Then I Daniel looked, and, behold, there stood other two *(men in Daniel's vision)*, the one on this side of the bank of the river, and the other on that side of the bank of the river.

And *one* said to the man clothed in linen, which *was* upon the waters of the river, How long *shall it be to* the end of these wonders?

The second, "time, times"

f And I heard the man clothed in linen, which *was* upon the waters of the river, when he held up his right hand and his left hand unto heaven, and sware by him that liveth for ever that *it shall be* **for a time, times, and an half; and when he (*God*) shall have accomplished to scatter the power *(knowledge of who God is)* of the holy people *(or saints of God)*, all these *things* shall be finished *(which shall culminate in the days of the second (2nd) coming of the Lord Jesus Christ).***

Daniel 11:45 – Daniel 12:7

Return to the Book of Revelation, Chapter 12 verse 10:

And I heard a loud voice saying in heaven, Now is come salvation, and strength, and the kingdom of our God, and the power of his Christ: for the accuser of our brethren is cast down, which accused them before our God day and night.

And they overcame him by the blood of the Lamb, and by the word of their testimony; and they loved not their lives unto the death.

Therefore rejoice, *ye* heavens, and ye that dwell in them. Woe to the inhabiters of the earth and of the sea! For the devil is come down unto you, having great wrath, because he knoweth that he hath but a short time.

And when the dragon saw that he was cast unto the earth, he persecuted the woman *(Israel)* which brought forth the man *(Jesus)*.

The third, "time, and times"

g And to the woman were given two wings of a great eagle, that she might fly into the wilderness, into her place, where she is nourished (sustained/ kept alive) **for a time, and times, and half a time *(which shall be the days of the second (2nd) coming of the Lord Jesus Christ)*,** from the face of the serpent.

And the serpent cast out of his mouth water *(criticisms, accusations, lies, bad press as water)* as a flood after the woman, that he might cause her to be carried away of the flood.

The end of, "time/ times"

h   And the woman *(Judah of Israel)* fled into the wilderness, where she hath a place prepared of God, that they *(the 144,000 and two witnesses)* should feed her *(or witness the Gospel of Jesus)* there **a thousand two hundred *and* threescore *(1260)* days *(3.452 years)*. This shall also be the time of the second *(2nd)* coming of the Lord Jesus Christ.**

Revelation 12:10 through 12:15 and Revelation 12:6

Relationship between the Man of Sin and Gog of Magog

The fate of the beast; world ruling power, the Man of Sin (Part 2)

And I saw the beast, and the kings of the earth, and their armies, gathered together to make war against him *(Jesus, King of kings)* that sat on the horse, and against his army *(saints, and angel of heaven)*.

And the beast *(man of sin)* was taken, and with him the false prophet that wrought miracles before him, with which he deceived them that had received the mark of the beast, and them that worshipped his image. These both were cast alive into a lake of fire burning with brimstone *(Also review Revelation Chapters 12 & 13)*.

Revelation 19:19 and 19:20

The fate of the Ruler, Gog of Magog (Ezekiel's Gog, Part 2)

Behold, it is come, and it is done, saith the Lord GOD; this is the day whereof I have spoken.

And they that dwell in the cities of Israel shall go forth, and shall set on fire and burn the weapons, both the shields and the bucklers, the bows and the arrows, and the handstaves, and the spears, and they shall burn them with fire seven *(7)* years:

So that they shall take no wood out of the field, neither cut down any out of the forests; for they shall burn the weapons with fire: and they shall spoil those that spoiled them, and rob those that robbed them, saith the Lord GOD.

And it shall come to pass in that day, that I will give unto Gog a place *(memorial?)* there of graves in Israel, the valley of the passengers *(passer-by, sightseer?)* on the east of the sea *(the Mediterranean)*: and it shall stop the noses of the passengers: and there shall they bury Gog and all his multitude: and they shall call it The valley of Hamongog. *(A place the sightseer would visit; a memorial park of graves; entire valley of nothing except grave markers?)*

Ezekiel 39:8 through 39:11

Summary Relationship of Ezekiel's Gog with the Man of Sin

I am persuaded that Gog of Magog and the man of sin is not the same individual because of *Revelation 19:20 and Ezekiel 39:11* in the previous two paragraphs. We see from these scriptures that God disposes each of them in a completely different manner. The man of sin shall be cast alive into a lake of fire burning with brimstone; which is the second *(2nd)* death.

But, Gog of Ezekiel's prophecy shall be given a place there of graves *(the first death)* in Israel, the valley of the passengers on the east of the sea *(the Mediterranean)*; and it shall stop the noses of the passengers: and there shall they bury Gog and all his multitude: and they shall call it The valley of Hamongog.

In addition those leaders of *"the ten horns/ nations"* are off-spring from times of old according to Daniel's description of the four beasts. But this end time individual we have been referring to as *"the man of sin"* shall come upon the world stage last; *subdue three of the ten (10) horn/ nations,* and establish his world kingdom authority as human authority's very last ruler. *However, the ultimate destination of both these personalities is the second (2nd) death as described in Revelation 19:20 & 19:21.*

I am also persuaded that Gog of Magog and the man of sin are of the fourth *(4th)* beast, or world ruling power as described in *Daniel Chapter 7*. This fourth *(4th)* beast of Daniel has *"ten horns/ nations"* in positions of great authority in the world *(Daniel Chapter 2 refers to the "ten horns/ nations" as "ten toes" in Nebuchadnezzar's dream because the four (4) world dominant kingdoms are described in the figure of a human statute having ten toes)*. It seems Gog of Magog may have his position of rule among these. However, it is not certain which of these *(Gog, or man of sin)* have the lesser position of authority, if they are in fact rulers at the same time in history.

But all of these *horns and\ or nations* will have one purpose toward Israel; which is total destruction. Hence, Jesus shall defend Israel against these enemies *(armies of the world)* at the *Battle of Armageddon* at his second *(2nd)* coming.

Since the *ten horns/ nations* grew out of *(having their ancestry from)* the time of the Roman Empire, the most *"Westerly Nations"* *(Americas, Canada, etc.)* might not be among the original ten *(10)* horns. However, the horn that had eyes *(the man of sin, and)* came up after the ten, and subdued three of the ten may very well have his roots in the Americas, or any other part of the world.

Daniel Chapter 7 verse 19:

Then I would know the truth of the fourth beast *(world ruling power)*, which was diverse from all the others *(three beasts)*, exceeding dreadful, whose teeth *were of* iron, and his nails *of* brass; *which* devoured, brake in pieces, and stamped the residue with his feet;

And of the ten horns *(nations)* that *were* in his *(the fourth beast's)* head, and *of* the other *(horn/ nation)* which came up, and before whom three *(of the original ten horns/ nations)* fell; even *of* that horn that had eyes, and a mouth that spake very great things, whose look *was* more stout than his fellows *(or other ten horns/ nations)*.

I beheld, and the same horn *(that had eyes)* made war with the saints, and prevailed against them;

Until *(a time and times and the dividing of time, and)* the Ancient of days came, and judgment was given to the saints of the most High; and the time came that the saints possessed the kingdom *(world ruling power)*.

Thus he *(the angel that talked with Daniel)* said, The fourth beast shall be the fourth kingdom *(world ruling power)* upon earth, which shall be diverse from all kingdoms, and shall devour the whole earth, and shall tread it down, and break it in pieces.

And the ten horns out of this kingdom *(world ruling power)* *are* ten kings *that* shall arise: and another *(horn)* shall rise after them; and he shall be diverse from the first, and he shall subdue three kings *(of the original ten)*.

And he shall speak *great* words against the most High *(God Almighty, Ancient of Days)*, and shall wear out the saints of the most High, and think to change times and laws: and they *(saints)* shall be given into his hand until **a time and times and the dividing of time** *(or, unto the end of kingdoms on earth, ruled by men)*.

But the judgment shall sit *(intervene; Jesus second coming)*, and they *(saints of the most High)* shall take away his *(the horn that had eyes)* dominion, to consume and to destroy *(his dominion)* unto the end *(of kingdoms ruled by men)*.

And the kingdom and dominion, and the greatness of the kingdom
under the whole heaven, shall be given to the people of the saints
of the most High, whose kingdom *is* an everlasting kingdom, and
all dominions shall serve and obey him *(the most High, Son of
God; Lord Jesus Christ)*.

Daniel 7:19 through 7:27

Book Summary

Let us take this opportunity to inventory some past prophetic events over the centuries concerning Judeo – Christian Bible Prophecy! The most obvious, and spectacular in recent years, even during the lifetime of many of our older citizens, which is *Judah of Israel (or the throne God promised King David)* would continue forever by the prophet Nathan *(See 2ⁿᵈ Samuel Chapter 7)*.

Fast forward to *1948 A.D. after World War II;* Israel *(or Judah of Israel)* became a *Nation State* again more than one and a half *(1 ½)* centuries after being destroyed by the Roman Empire in seventy *(70) A.D.)*!

One would think this alone would go the necessary distance in convincing the most *"hard of believing individual"* of the reality of God our Creation, and His instructions *(the Judeo – Christian Bible)* for the human race!

But let us suppose all are still not yet convinced.

So then, let us consider the warnings the LORD God gave through Moses for the situation(s) when Israel wandered away from Him into the camps of false gods and idols.

Deuteronomy Chapter 29

If Israel does not continue in the commandments of the LORD God they shall be plucked out of their land! These are words of the covenant being added along with the covenant that was made at Horeb near the Mountain Sinai! The LORD God did many signs and wonders (or miracles) when He brought the children of Israel out of Egypt by the hand of Moses.

These *are* the words of the covenant, which the LORD commanded Moses to make with the children of Israel in the land of Moab, beside the covenant which he made with them in Horeb *(near Sinai)*.

And Moses called unto all Israel, and said unto them, Ye have seen all that the LORD did before your eyes in the land of Egypt unto Pharaoh, and unto all his servants, and unto all his land;

The great temptations which thine eyes have seen, the signs, and those great miracles:

Yet the LORD hath not given you an heart to perceive, and eyes to
see, and ears to hear, unto this day *(It seems Moses is saying
here: Even though you have experienced and seen with your
own eyes the many things the LORD God has performed
amongst us; you have yet to grasp hold of the full purpose of
what God is doing concerning Israel)*.

Deuteronomy 29:1 through 29:4

*But it is the LORD God that has kept Israel, and if they abandon
Him for idols and false gods, He shall not spare, or show pity for
them!*

And I *(the LORD God)* have led you forty *(40)* years in the
wilderness: your clothes are not waxen old upon you, and thy
shoe is not waxen old upon thy foot.

Ye have not eaten bread, neither have ye drunk wine or strong drink:
that ye might know that I *am* the LORD your God *(that has kept
Israel)*.

And when ye came unto this place, Sihon the king of Heshbon, and
Og the king of Bashan, came out against us unto battle, and we
smote them:

And we took their land, and gave it for an inheritance unto the
Reubenites, and to the Gadites, and to the half tribe of Manasseh.

Keep therefore the words of this covenant, and do them, that ye may
prosper in all that ye do.

Ye stand this day all of you before the LORD your God; your
captains of your tribes, your elders, and your officers, *with* all the
men of Israel,

Your little ones, your wives, and thy stranger that *is* in thy camp,
from the hewer of thy wood unto the drawer of thy water:

That thou shouldest enter into covenant with the LORD thy God, and
into his oath, which the LORD thy God maketh with thee this
day:

That he may establish thee to day for a people unto himself, and *that*
he may be unto thee a God, as he hath said unto thee, and as he
hath sworn unto thy fathers, to Abraham, to Isaac, and to Jacob.

Neither with you only do I make this covenant and this oath;

But with *him* that standeth here with us this day before the LORD
our God, and also with *him* that *is* not here with us this day:

(For ye know how we have dwelt in the land of Egypt; and how we
    came through the nations which ye passed by;
And ye have seen their abominations *(sin and iniquities in
    worshipping that which is not God)*, and their idols *(of)*, wood
    and stone, silver and gold, which *were* among them:)
Lest *(or with the intention to prevent)* there should be among you
    man, or woman, or family, or tribe, whose heart turneth away
    this day from the LORD our God, to go *and* serve the gods of
    these *(other)* nations; lest *(or with the intention to prevent)* there
    should be among you a root that beareth gall and wormwood;
And it come to pass, when he *(that that will not obey
    commandments of the LORD God)* heareth the words of this
    curse, that he bless himself in his heart, saying, I shall have
    peace, though I walk in the imagination of mine heart, to add
    drunkenness to thirst:
The LORD will not spare him, but then the anger of the LORD and
    his jealousy shall smoke against that man, and all the curses that
    are written in this book shall lie upon him, and the LORD shall
    blot out his name from under heaven.
And the LORD shall separate him unto evil out of all the tribes of
    Israel, according to all the curses of the covenant that are written
    in this book of the law:
So that the generation to come of your children that shall rise up
    after you, and the stranger that shall come from a far land, shall
    say, when they see the plagues of that land, and the sicknesses
    which the LORD hath laid upon it;
And that the whole land thereof *is* brimstone, and salt, *and* burning,
    that it is not sown, nor beareth, nor any grass groweth therein,
    like the overthrow of Sodom, and Gomorrah, Admah, and
    Zeboim, which the LORD overthrew in his anger, and in his
    wrath:
Even all nations shall say, Wherefore hath the LORD done thus unto
    this land *(Israel)*? what *meaneth* the heat of this great anger?
Then men shall say, Because they have forsaken the covenant of the
    LORD God of their fathers, which he made with them when he
    brought them forth out of the land of Egypt:
For they went and served other gods, and worshipped them, gods
    whom they knew not, and *whom* he *(God)* had not given unto
    them:

And the anger of the LORD was kindled against this land, to bring
upon it all the curses that are written in this book:
And the LORD rooted them out of *(or plucked Israel up from)* their
land in anger, and in wrath, and in great indignation
(displeasure), and cast *(or scattered)* them into another land, as *it
is* this day.
The secret *things belong* unto the LORD our God: but those *things
which are* revealed *belong* unto us and to our children for ever,
that *we* may do all the words of this law.

Deuteronomy 29:5 through 29:29

Deuteronomy Chapter 30

***But the LORD God shall gather the children of Israel into the land
again after He will have scattered them throughout the nation of
the world, because of their "false god\ idol worship, and iniquity"!***
And it shall come to pass, when all these things are come upon thee,
the blessing and the curse, which I have set before thee, and thou
shalt call *them* to mind among all the nations, whither the LORD
thy God hath driven thee *(or scattered thee!)*,
And shalt return *(after many years?)* unto the LORD thy God, and
shalt obey his voice according to all that I command thee this
day, thou and thy children, with all thine heart, and with all thy
soul;
That then the LORD thy God will turn thy captivity *(or bring you,
Israel, into the land again)*, and have compassion upon thee, and
will return and gather thee from all the nations, whither the
LORD thy God hath scattered thee.
If *any* of thine *(the people of Israel)* be driven out unto the outmost
parts of heaven *(for a season)*, from thence will the LORD thy
God gather thee, and from thence will he fetch thee:
And the LORD thy God will bring thee into the land which thy
fathers possessed, and thou shalt possess it; and he will do thee
good, and multiply thee above thy fathers.
And the LORD thy God will circumcise thine heart, and the heart of
thy seed *(or offspring)*, to love the LORD thy God with all thine
heart, and with all thy soul, that thou mayest live.

Deuteronomy 30:1 through 30:6

Then the LORD God shall punish the enemies of Israel! And then Israel shall obey the voice of the LORD God and do all His commandments!

And the LORD thy God will put all these curses upon thine enemies, and on them that hate thee, which persecuted thee.

And thou shalt return and obey the voice of the LORD, and do all his commandments which I command thee this day.

And the LORD thy God will make thee plenteous in every work of thine hand, in the fruit of thy body, and in the fruit of thy cattle, and in the fruit of thy land, for good: for the LORD will again rejoice over thee for good, as he rejoiced over thy fathers:

If thou shalt hearken unto the voice of the LORD thy God, to keep his commandments and his statutes which are written in this book of the law, *and* if thou turn unto the LORD thy God with all thine heart, and with all thy soul.

For this commandment which I command thee this day, it *is* not hidden from thee, neither *is* it far off.

It *is* not in heaven, that thou shouldest say, Who shall go up for us to heaven, and bring it unto us, that we may hear it, and do it?

Neither *is* it beyond the sea, that thou shouldest say, Who shall go over the sea for us, and bring it unto us, that we may hear it, and do it?

But the word *is* very nigh unto thee, in thy mouth, and in thy heart, that thou mayest do it *(also see Romans 10:6 through 10:10)*.

See, I have set before thee this day life and good, and death and evil;

In that I command thee this day to love the LORD thy God, to walk in his ways, and to keep his commandments and his statutes and his judgments, that thou mayest live and multiply: and the LORD thy God shall bless thee in the land whither thou goest to possess it.

Deuteronomy 30:7 through 30:16

The results of abandoning the LORD God; and for us today: never ever having come to Him!

But if thine heart turn away, so that thou wilt not hear, but shalt be drawn away, and worship other gods, and serve them *(idols and false gods)*;

I denounce unto you this day, that ye shall surely perish, *and that* ye
   shall not prolong *your* days upon the land, whither thou passest
   over Jordan to go to possess it.
I call heaven and earth to record this day against you, *that* I have set
   before you life and death, blessing and cursing: therefore choose
   life, that both thou and thy seed may live:
That thou mayest love the LORD thy God, *and* that thou mayest
   obey his voice, and that thou mayest cleave unto him: for he *is*
   thy life, and the length of thy days: that thou mayest dwell in the
   land which the LORD sware unto thy fathers, to Abraham, to
   Isaac, and to Jacob, to give them.

Deuteronomy 30:17 through 30:20

*Israel lost her way on more than one occasion; then as a result
there came a time when God allowed her enemies to have their way
over and against her; removing the people from their homeland
inheritance (and making them desolate).*
*The longest desolation has been after the 70 A.D. destruction by
the Romans. But today, God has brought them into their homeland
again, as He promised, after more than (1 ½) centuries!*
*And we not only have the Judeo – Christian Bible record of how or
when so many Bible prophecies have already come to pass, but
secular history also plays a role in verifying fulfilled Judeo –
Christian Bible Prophecy! All we need do is consider the Old
Testament Prophets; especially Daniel, Isaiah, Jeremiah, Ezekiel,
Ezra, Nehemiah; the Books of 2nd Samuel, 1st & 2nd Kings, and the
New Testament Gospels. The entire record of what we should
expect is provided from Genesis unto Revelation!*
*So why would anyone be so foolish to dismiss, and think "end of
end time prophecies (the Book of Revelation)" could never come to
pass?*

Definitions & Figures

Apocrypha Books – Perhaps the argument can be made that the commandment from Moses, in the ***Book of Deuteronomy, Verses 17:14 through 17:20*** might be a contributing factor to the productions of so many "stand alone" Judeo – Christian works that were not included with the official, "Canon of Scripture"! Such writings have been assigned the category of, ***"Apocrypha Books"***. Even though the commandment is specifically for the king of Israel, Moses does not exclude any other persons ***(whether just curious, dedicated, or otherwise)*** about God; from attempting the very same task of copying scripture texts! For example, there are a few Psalms not written by the king!

But the Holy Spirit superintended, and had final say of the writings that constitute the Canon of Scripture available for us today, which consist of the Old and New Testaments ***(described primarily by the King James, and documentations used to develop the King James (i.e., the King James seems to be the most widely used). Zechariah 4:6 is one of our many witnesses in scripture that God bring to past what He does by His Spirit; the Holy Spirit)***!

When the people of Israel decided they wanted a king in Israel, rather than the LORD God in single authority over them:

When thou art come unto the land which the LORD thy God giveth thee, and shalt possess it, and shalt dwell therein, and shalt say, I will set a king over me, like as all the nations that *are* about me ***(by the way the nations round about them were false god and idol worshippers; or heathens!)***;

Thou shalt in any wise set *him* king over thee, whom the LORD thy God shall choose: *one* from among thy brethren shalt thou set king over thee: thou mayest not set a stranger over thee, which *is* not thy brother ***(or not from the line of Jacob)***.

But he shall not multiply horses to himself, nor cause the people to return to Egypt, to the end that he should multiply horses: forasmuch as the LORD hath said unto you, Ye shall henceforth return no more that way ***(to Egypt, which are worshippers of many false gods and idols)***.

Neither shall he multiply wives to himself, that his heart turn not away ***(from the LORD God of his fathers; Abraham, Isaac, and***

Jacob): neither shall he greatly multiply to himself silver and gold *(that he turns away from trusting the LORD God)*.

And it shall be, when he sitteth upon the throne of his kingdom, that he shall write him a copy of this law in a book out of *that which is* before the priests the Levites *(in other words the King in Israel shall write his own copy of the Bible, <u>based upon,</u> or using the existing books that is with the priesthood)*:

And it *(the copy of his (the Kings) Bible that he writes)* shall be with him, and he shall read therein all the days of his life: that he may learn to fear the LORD his God, to keep all the words of this law and these statutes, to do them:

That his heart be not lifted up above his brethren *(or those he is king over)*, and that he turn not aside from the commandment, *to* the right hand, or *to* the left: to the end that he may prolong *his* days in his kingdom, he, and his children, in the midst of Israel.

Deuteronomy 17:14 through 17:20

Dispensations – There are Seven *(7)* <u>**Primary**</u> Dispensations, which can be described as imbedded with Judeo – Christian Bible Scripture. We have been living in the "Dispensation *(6)* of Grace" for the past *1988 years*! This calculation is determined by the current year *(2022 A.D.)* minus the year *(34 A.D.)* since the crucifixion and resurrection of Jesus!

Many others before yours truly have said much on the subject of Biblical Dispensations. It is one of those concepts that most well meaning Christians would say, "Dispensation(s)?" why, it is not mentioned in Judeo – Christian Scripture! And they would be correct.

However, I contend it is born out of Bible witness, and permits the dedicated Bible student to recognize the stages of the process the LORD God has continued use of for creating the human race in His likeness as described in *Genesis 1:26 through Genesis 1:28*! And even today, the process is ongoing; being spread out over thousands of years, since Adam!

And let us also say it this way: The concept of Bible Dispensations is inherent information of knowledge *(i.e., understanding)* of Bible Scripture revealed by the *Holy Spirit*; much like the word "Rapture" not appearing in written Judeo – Christian Bible Text! But we understand and know by Bible study and analysis; the *Holy Spirit* working with us to see Biblical Truths; that "Rapture" has the meaning of, "catching away of Saints by the *Lord Jesus Christ*"! Some modern day Bible Scholars\ Teachers\ Men of God agree that there shall be seven *(7)* Dispensations and then the human race will have begun the, "Perfect Age of FOREVER, or Eternal Living"!

Initial Creation of the Man Adam in the Image of God

Gen 1:26 And God said, Let us make man in our image, after our likeness: and let them have dominion over the fish of the sea, and over the fowl of the air, and over the cattle, and over all the earth, and over every creeping thing that crept upon the earth.

Gen 1:27 So God created man *(Adam)* in his own image, in the image of God created he him; male and female created he them *(Adam and Eve)*.

Gen 1:28 And God blessed them, and God said unto them, be fruitful, and multiply, and replenish the earth, and subdue it: and have dominion over the fish of the sea, and over the fowl of the air, and over every living thing that moved upon the earth.

And so we see that God created the man Adam! But it turned out the creation of Adam was only the beginning of God creating man *(human kind)* in His image; after His likeness, because Adam sinned *(and Dear friends, God does not sin!)*.
Thus, man fell from the image God created him, which was the image of God; after the likeness of God!
Now, since God knows everything and nothing surprises Him can we say God knew Adam would fall? And therefore require additional steps\ processes\ stages of development to finally get man *(the human race)* created in His image and likeness.
Therefore, *"Dispensation(s)"* of necessity are manifest; or stages of God dealing with creating man in His image over thousands of years; and requiring many generations, that there not be any fall when He is done! And so, I am persuaded the reasons God chose to continue recovery of man unto Himself *(His image\ after His likeness\ His eternalness)* is that His word not be broken, and because of *"His Great Love"*.

There are modern day Bible Scholars\ Teachers\ Men of God that agree there shall be ***seven (7) Primary Dispensations*** and then the human race will have begun the, "Perfect Age of FOREVER, or Eternal Living"!

The sixth *(6th)* Dispensation:
Our present day Dispensation is the ***Dispensation of Grace*** because Jesus *(being the perfect obedient Son of God and son of man)* sacrificed Himself to pay the sin debt of all human kind ever akin to God. ***However, it saddens me to say "all human kind have not in the past, nor presently, take advantage of the gift and sacrifice of Jesus".***
Promises from God are now given, through His Mercy and Grace *(Jesus Christ)*, for every *human creature*; their sins forgiven *(Halleluiah; Halleluiah; Halleluiah, and Amen)*! And His offer of

forgiveness includes eternal living before *(or in)* His presence, when we believes His promises; asking for forgiveness of our sins in the name of Jesus!

This present Dispensation has continued since the resurrection of Jesus, which have been approximately, ***"1988 years (or 2022 A.D. minus 34 A.D.; the time of the resurrection of Jesus)"***!

Dispensation (6) of Grace also began in the middle of the last week of Daniel's seventieth *(70th)* week, or at **69 ½ Weeks**!

The Son of God; ***Jesus,*** who is also the son of man, because He was born of the virgin, Mary, to die in sacrifice for the sins of the human race! And the LORD God was pleased to see His sacrifice from the foundation of the world!

Jesus brought the ***New Covenant*** with Him; accomplishing His purpose through ***Covenant Sacrifice*** planned of His Father from foundation of the world!

The Primary elements of His ***Covenant*** are forgiveness of sin, and eternal life in an incorruptible body of the kind He *(Jesus)* returned from the dead with, at His resurrection!

Dispensation *(6)* of Grace has the ***"Resurrection Rapture"*** of the saints *(or the Church)* as the next milestone ***(which shall be even more awesomely spectacular than as Noah's Flood)***, which shall occur as described in ***Revelation Chapter 6:12 through 7:17.*** And it would seem this Dispensation *(6)* of Grace continues through Tribulation events of ***Revelation Chapters 8 through 19.*** Then, according to ***Revelation Chapter 20:1 through 20:6,*** Dispensation *(7)* of Righteousness & Peace begins and continues a thousand *(1000)* years!

During the thousand *(1000)* years of Dispensation *(7)*, Satan shall be bound in the bottomless pit, ***while Jesus reigns in Righteousness and Peace***!

Today, this Dispensation of Grace *(the sixth (6th) Dispensation)* brings us to about ***6200 years*** of the ***"human creation process"*** unto the likeness of God, since the creation of Adam. And the process shall continue until fulfilled, when Jesus appears the second *(2nd)* time on the Planet!

The fifth *(5th)* Dispensation:
The previous *(or fifth (5th))* Dispensation was the "Dispensation of Law", which speaks of the perfect will of the LORD God set in

place; passing His Commandments by *Covenant to Israel through Moses* that they should live by them *(Commandments)*, and evangelize the world of their day of Him *(God)*, by them *(Laws\ Commandments from the LORD God)*; the True God of Heaven and Creation.

But we know Israel stumbled severely on two *(2)* primary occasions; resulting in the ten *(10)* Northern Tribes of Samaria ceasing to be a Nation forever, at the hands of Assyrian defeat in *722 B.C.*! And the second occasion of their stumbling was the Southern Tribes *(Judah, Benjamin, and Simeon*) at Jerusalem became captives in *586 B.C.* by Babylon's Nebuchadnezzar, and they were exiled for *70 years* until the LORD God brought them into their land of promise again *(but Northern Israel never recovered as a Nation)*!

The LORD God sent prophet after prophet *(beginning with the prophet Elijah)*; warning them to come away from false god and idol worship, and recommit to Him *(the only true God of Heaven & Creation, and the God of their Fathers)*!

This fifth *(5ᵗʰ)* Dispensation continued for about *1500 years* before ours today; the sixth *(6ᵗʰ)* Dispensation of Grace began! It is accepted that this is also the beginning event of the Church Age, which was at the Acts Chapter two *(2)* infilling of the *Holy Sprit*; after resurrection from the dead, and ascension of Christ Jesus into Heaven again!

Then the most recent and severest stumbling of Israel *(or Judah of Israel; the remnant of Israel; recovered from Babylonian exile)* was their rejection of Jesus; Messiah:

As this Dispensation *(5)* of Law was coming to a close, God sent His Son Jesus *(with the New Covenant)*! And New Testament Judeo - Christians Gospels provides detailed accounts of His Birth, Ministry, Sacrifice *(or death)*, and Resurrection from the dead to life again!

It is at the very close of this Dispensation *(5)*; that Jesus having received the *Holy Spirit without measure* from His Father in Heaven; during the event of His John the Baptist baptism by water; in turn sent the Holy Spirit on Pentecost to His followers *(the Church)* after His death, resurrection, and ascension into Heaven!

The first four *(4)* Dispensations were lived out during past generations beginning with Adam, and our descriptions are as provided below:

- The Dispensation *(1)* of Innocence, continued less that *100 years,* or ended when Adam sinned

Gen 2:7 And the LORD God formed man *of* the dust of the ground, and breathed into his nostrils the breath of life; and man became a living soul.

Every other creature the LORD God created as described in Genesis Chapter 1 was not breathed into; only the man was breathed into! And so, we see God purposed to put something of Himself into the man, which caused man to become a breathing living soul. Therefore, as near as we are able to determined no other creature of Genesis Chapter 1 has a "soul"!

Also refer to the paragraph in titled, **"The Kinsman Redeemer"** and related paragraphs in this **"Definitions & Figures"** section.

- The Dispensation *(2)* of Conscience, began after Adam's sin and continued about *1600 years,* or until the flood of Noah ended, which the LORD God delivered Noah and his family to safety

Men then and now knew the difference between good and evil; and yet chose not to honor God by doing good, but indulged in evil to the extent their minds were on evil continually *(much like today)*. Thus, the reason God sent the Flood upon the Earth during the time of Noah, whom God declared righteous, because Noah believed in God. And it was after the Flood in this Dispensation *(2)* the LORD God introduced *"Covenant"* to Noah and his seed, declaring that He would not destroy the Earth by flood again!

- The Dispensation *(3)* of Government, continued about *500 years;* beginning after the flood, and until the death of Noah and his son Shem

Immediately after the Flood and for a time, Noah and his family were the only human creatures on the Planet. And it would seem the only land animal creatures were of those that Noah brought with him in the Ark! And so, this was the first time, since Adam, the LORD God began another population of human kind on the Planet, whose minds were not on evil continually! The next time this type of effort is scheduled to take place, shall be when Jesus appears the second

(2ⁿᵈ) time, and the "Dispensation *(7)* of Righteousness & Peace" continues for a thousand *(1000)* years!

- The Dispensation *(4)* of Promise, continued about *500 to 600 years;* beginning with Abraham, and continuing until Moses

And its beginning is usually agreed to be the time God spoke to Abraham about blessing him through *Covenant Promise* with a son according to faith, grace and promise! Therefore, Abraham's offspring resulting from this son of *Covenant Promise\ Faith & Grace* would be blessed of God forever! And not only would Abraham's progeny receive blessings, but the whole world also!

And so, we see the purpose of God in blessing, was not just for Abraham and his offspring alone, but the whole Gentile world too should be blessed, throughout eternity!

It is during the time of this Dispensation *(4)* the LORD God reveals the level of importance He places on Birthright, which speaks to the method God uses to pass *"Covenant Promises Inherited"* to the next generation.

Since *Esau* being the eldest of Isaac's two *(2) covenant sons (Esau & Jacob)* did not place much importance on his Birthright *(or being first born)*, God allowed the Birthright inheritance to pass to Jacob; whom he *(Jacob)* did very much appreciate the things of God!

This Dispensation *(4)* of Promise was overtaken by the Dispensation *(5)* of Law when God called Moses to Ministry; leading the *Covenant People*, Israel of promise out of Egyptian bondage *(having become about 6,000,000 in number).*

The seventh *(7ᵗʰ)* and final Dispensation shall be the "Dispensation of Righteousness & Peace", when Jesus shall return *(or appear the second (2ⁿᵈ))* time and rule the Earth, just as in Heaven for a thousand *(1000) years*! There shall be Great Tribulation from God at His initial return, as He solidify\ consolidate\ establish His reign upon the Planet. We can expect those events as *"prophesied and described"* in the Book of Revelation to occur!

See Revelation Chapter 20:4 through 20:6.

And when the thousand *(1000)* years are expired, Satan shall be loosed out of his prison,

Those that lived during the thousand (1000) years of the Dispensation (7) of Righteousness & Peace had no deception\ temptation(s). But now that Satan is loosed to deceive the Nations,

*the evaluation of their sincerity to be with Christ Jesus is revealed,
as Satan is now present with his deception(s)!*

And *(he; Satan)* shall go out to deceive the nations which are in the
four *(4)* quarters of the earth, Gog and Magog *(this army of Gog,
and Magog is another generation of Gog and Magog than that
of Ezekiel Chapters 38 and 39)*, to gather them together to battle
*(**not** the battle of Armageddon; but the battle as described in
these next verses)*: the number of whom *is* as the sand of the sea.

And they went up on the breadth of the earth, and compassed the
camp of the saints about, and the beloved city *(Jerusalem)*: and
fire came down from God out of heaven, and devoured them
*(this is a very, very, very … short battle; the LORD God just
simply consumed them with fire in a fraction of time! The
Dispensation (6) of Grace was overtaken at the beginning of
the Dispensation (7) of Righteousness & Peace (i.e., the 1000
years. Therefore, no source of mercy\ grace was available to be
afforded those of this Gog\ Magog army)*.

And the devil that deceived them was cast into the lake of fire and
brimstone, where the beast and the false prophet *are,* and shall be
tormented day and night for ever and ever.

Revelation 20:7 through 20:10

Our Personal Dispensation

I am persuaded a logical conclusion about Dispensations is that each
of us has our own *"personal dispensation"*! We know it as living
this lifetime *(which is less than one hundred (100) years for most
folks)*! And during our *personal dispensation* the LORD God
expects us to discover the Wisdom that is Him; and that we embrace
Him for more life according to the method He has set in place
through His Son, Jesus the Christ and savior of the human race! It is
by the *Holy Spirit* He has seen to it that we have His Book *(His
Word)*; the Judeo – Christian Bible, so that we can make right
decision(s). *This is what life is all about, FIRST. But it is our
decision to want it according to His requirement(s)*. And I'm
persuaded He knows that we are *able* to figure it out and choose
right *(John 3:16)*; discarding the wrong! After all, since He created
us, He knows what we are capable of! Amen!

Heathen - Or No Covenant With the Eternal God: *I am persuaded the meaning of this word has no real lasting use and/ or value unless it is viewed from the eyes of the Real and True God of Creation! Any other view has no lasting impact and meaning, because it shall die forever with the person, or persons view point that is "heathen"; especially if the True Creator's evaluation instruction(s) is not accepted, and embraced. And so, the "heathen" in the sight of the True God and Creator is anyone that does not have Him (God) in their life and living!*

But from the perspective of souls that do not believe there is a One True God, or erroneously believe that their particular deity is God the following meaning may be applied:

Heathen people(s) collectively, and especially (in the use of one's "holy book"; *if one exists*) are those who did not *(or does not)* worship the God of their fathers:

Where the God of Israel is concerned, this would be the God of the Judeo – Christian Bible; which God is also the God of Abraham, Isaac, and Jacob, according to Covenant.

And so, everyone today has available this dilemma (<u>whether they think it important or not</u>) of giving consideration to the offering of <u>Jesus the Messiah and Christ</u>, according to John 3:16, as described in the Judeo – Christian Holy Bible Books. The other choices are to follow after anything else contrary to the Judeo – Christian Bible Doctrine!

Thus, everyone chooses; and the Judeo – Christine Scriptures makes the following clear: Whosoever will believe the Gospel of Jesus Christ "SHALL" be saved, and enter life that is eternal with the True God of Creation, and Jesus Christ the Savior! Amen.

Judeo – Christian Bible Covenants – The scriptures does not speak of Adam having covenant with God, but we know He had *"fellowship"* until his sin separated him from God! Thus, I am persuaded a covenant relationship may be beneath Adam's original relationship with God? *But the LORD God never breaks covenant, which covenant shares appropriately with all included!*

And so, we see that God did not formally *(or by record)* obligate Himself to the safety and well being of the human race again *(after Adam sinned)* until Noah, and the decision that He would destroy the earth *(or perhaps saying it this way is more meaningful: earth's population(s) did whatever they pleased without having any concern of what God wanted; just as the dog, and vast numbers of <u>none believing</u> folks today)*!

And from the time of Noah, if the LORD God were to save any out of the human race He would need to bring them unto Him once again to such a state as before Adam sinned!

Thus, the LORD God instituted *"covenant"*; of which, the final state of covenant needed to be everlasting, with that of the ***Lord Jesus Christ; His Son, who is Himself, "everlasting"***!

Covenant with God has within it *(**UNDESERVED, AND ABSENT OF THE SINFUL**: elements; attributes of mercy\ forgiveness\ favors\ grace\ love\ joy\ peace\ longsuffering\ goodness ..., and just all around necessary stuff(s))* whereby the ***LORD God of Creation*** may forgive violations against Him *(and His Law(s))*!

Thus, the key element of the ***final covenant***; of necessity being the ***Son of God sacrificed***; the ***LORD Jesus Christ*** filled with, and possessing these covenant attributes\ qualities\ elements! And the Father assigns these to the forgiven in ***Christ Jesus*** for ***righteousness***.

But the <u>first *(1ˢᵗ)* covenant was with Noah</u> to save ***all*** in the Ark ***alive*** through the flood that destroyed the earth. And that covenant included the promise of God to every earth creature that He would not destroy the earth again by water of a flood *(or the climate?)!* The ***LORD God*** <u>extended this covenant with Noah and his progeny, to Abraham and his progeny</u>, and ***adjusted the covenant*** to include more promises for blessing those that He would save throughout the centuries unto salvation by the ***Lord Jesus Christ; Messiah***!

Gen 28:14 And thy *(Abraham's)* seed shall be as the dust of the earth, and thou shalt spread abroad to the west, and to the east, and to the north, and to the south: and in thee and in thy seed shall all the families of the earth be blessed.

By close examination we see that elements of this covenant with Abraham also spoke to the fulfilling of salvation that would be accomplished by the final ***"Covenant Son, Jesus Christ; the Messiah"***!

And this final covenant is initiated with Jesus being infilled, (without measure; John 3:30 through 3:34) with the Holy Spirit at His John the Baptist baptism:

Matthew Chapter 3

In those days came John the Baptist, preaching in the wilderness of Judaea,

And saying, Repent ye: for the kingdom of heaven is at hand.

For this is he that was spoken of by the prophet Esaias *(Isaiah)*, saying, The voice of one crying in the wilderness, Prepare ye the way of the Lord, make his paths straight *(This is the prophecy of Isaiah 40:3 through 40:8, and Judah of Israel was instructed what they were to do in Isaiah 40:9 and 40:10)*.

And the same John *(the Baptist)* had his raiment of camel's hair, and a leathern girdle about his loins; and his meat was locusts and wild honey.

Then went out to him *(John the Baptist)* Jerusalem, and all Judaea, and all the region round about Jordan,

And were baptized of him in Jordan, confessing their sins.

But when he saw many of the Pharisees and Sadducees come to his baptism, he said unto them, O generation of vipers, who hath warned you to flee from the wrath to come? *(See "Pharisees" in the "Definitions & Figures" section)*

Bring forth therefore fruits meet *(or suitable)* for repentance:

And think not to say within yourselves, We have Abraham to our father: for I say unto you, that God is able of these stones to raise up children unto Abraham.

And now also the axe is laid unto the root of the trees: therefore every tree which bringeth not forth good fruit is hewn down, and cast into the fire *(The implication here is that the previous covenant, which was violated of Israel time and time again is being replaced! And is in process of being taken away even now at the coming of Messiah; Jesus? And violation of the previous covenant is obvious when studying Old Testament Scriptures!)*.

Today we know, "He", being referred to in these next scriptures is the Lord Jesus Christ; Messiah!

I *(John the Baptist)* indeed baptize you with water unto repentance:
but he that cometh after me is mightier than I, whose shoes I am
not worthy to bear: he shall baptize you with the Holy Ghost *(or
Holy Spirit)*, and *with* fire:
Whose fan *is* in his hand *(to separate the chaff from the wheat)*, and
he will throughly purge his floor, and gather his wheat into the
garner; but he will burn up the chaff with unquenchable fire.

Matthew 3:1 through 3:12

The <u>next major covenant</u> event of the Old Testament also passed
down, from Abraham to Moses was by inheritance too. *This
covenant was adjustment* to extend through Moses in order to free
from Egyptian slavery, unto a land promised the seed of Abraham.
This seed of Abraham began with the Nation of People *(or Israel)*,
which God established during the years of Isaac *(the covenant son
from God to Abraham and Sarah)*; Jacob *(son of Isaac and
Rebekah)*, and Joseph *(son of Jacob and Rachel)*.
And again elements of this covenant *(especially Passover,
Sacrificing and Offering, which was trusted with the Levitical
Priesthood)* also spoke, specifically, to the fulfilling of salvation that
would be accomplished by the *"Final Covenant Son, Jesus Christ;
the Messiah"*, and His one *(1)* time sacrifice of His own life, which
life is offered to the world for them that ***believe*** according to *John
3:16*!

Then King David *(son of Jesse; in Jacob's progeny of the tribe of
JUDAH is given first birthright inheritance)* being an inheritor of
the covenants passed down before him by the status of a covenant
progeny; was singled out of God unto the *adjusted covenant
condition* for receiving blessings of his throne continuing forever
(Refer to, "Thy Throne Forever" in the "Definitions & Figures")
section!

Next, True Holy men and Prophets of God being inheritors of all the
covenants, through the centuries *(beginning with Noah's covenant)*;
and before the *final new eternal life covenant of Jesus*, were tasked
of the *LORD God* to inform the world of their day of the
approaching eternal salvation covenant through *Jesus, the Messiah
(Daniel the prophet being given one of the most honored positions*

of notoriety, because he showed precise timings of Jesus appearing and filled with the Holy Spirit, crucifixion, resurrection, and ascension into heaven again)!

And so, <u>concerning us today</u>, everyone gets to choose whether to accept, and be in covenant with God through *Jesus Christ; Messiah*, according to *John 3:16: Which meaning is, "God so loved that He gave His Son", and the ongoing effort through the centuries is to accomplish the receiving of the gift by the human race, to whom the gift was intended: And the gift being, "the human race is forgiven of sin; infilled with the Holy Spirit; and life eternal with God"!*

But I am persuaded it is not pleasing to the *LORD God* of Heaven and Creation, that many, many people continues to rejects *Jesus, who is described in John 3:16*; and\ or chooses to do their living under behaviors of previous covenants, that *"pointed to",* but had not the *"fulfilled elements"* promised with eternal life!

And there are also those that do not choose to seek life with the *True God of Creation*, at all!

The Kinsman Redeemer – The LORD God instructed Moses to implement the principle describing the "Kinsman Redeemer" into the law and commandments to Israel.

This speaks of one having much seeing his kinsman with little, or no means to help himself, even to the extent of not having what is needed to continue day to day living. And the kinsman with much *"choose as his responsibility"* to meet the redeeming needs of his kinsman *(See Deuteronomy Chapter 15)*!

The primary message of the Book of Ruth describes the Kinsman Redeemer through the relationship of Boaz and Ruth.

Obviously Boaz, the kinsman redeemer of Ruth is a type of the Lord Jesus Christ not only redeeming Israel at His first visitation in the world, but Jesus is the ultimate Kinsman Redeemer that redeems "whosoever will" unto the Father according to *John 3:16!*

Recall what the LORD God instructed Moses to write in Genesis 1:26 and 1:27:

Gen 1:26 And God said, Let us make man in our image, after our
   likeness: and let them have dominion over the fish of the sea, and

over the fowl of the air, and over the cattle, and over all the
earth, and over every creeping thing that creepeth upon the earth.
Gen 1:27 So God created man in his *own* image, in the image of
God created he him; male and female created he them.

***Bible researchers speculate this occurred about Six Thousand Two
Hundred (6200) Years Ago: The Creation of Adam <u>(Man in the
image of God; never done before</u>!? Thus, man is created one
hundred (100) percent man, and akin to God!?)***

But then Physical Life continued, without Life of the Spirit after the
man, Adam sinned against God in disobedience– Genesis Chapter 3
forward …

And so, relationship between God and man can be made right again;
but only if there is a "Kinsman Redeemer" to complete the
redemption!

**In my mind the implication here spawn answers to several
questions as follows:**

- There is no missing link between **<u>any</u>** prehistory creature and
  this man, Adam that is akin to God; ***<u>and therefore
  redeemable (or can be brought back!)</u>***? Thus, the dog is not
  redeemable; there can be another one, but not the same one,
  ever! And so, any person ***rejecting John 3:16 (although
  redeemable)*** achieve the unredeemable state as the dog? And
  the finality of their living shall be that of grass in the field, as
  described by Isaiah Chapter 40:6 through 40:8!

Mat 7:6 Give not that which is holy unto the dogs, neither cast ye
your pearls before swine, lest they trample them under their
feet, and turn again and rend you.

Mat 15:26 But he answered and said, It is not meet to take the
children's bread, and to cast *it* to dogs.

Mat 15:27 And she said, Truth, Lord: yet the dogs eat of the
crumbs which fall from their masters' table.

- ***The Holy Spirit of God commanded manifestation of God
  the Son, Jesus in the flesh, whereby the fallen may become
  redeemed Son of Adam; and therefore akin to God? Thus,
  Jesus had to be (of necessity); one hundred (100) percent
  man, and one hundred (100) percent God?***

- No one shall ever compile a list of all the attributes of the Eternal Almighty God whereby it may be determined, how much of Himself God put in Adam, and therefore the human race?

1Jn 3:2 Beloved, now are we the sons of God, and it doth not yet appear what we shall be: but we know that, when he shall appear, we shall be like him; for we shall see him as he is.

- Is there anything too hard for the LORD, or is there anything impossible with the LORD God?

Jer 32:17 Ah Lord GOD! behold, thou hast made the heaven and the earth by thy great power and stretched out arm, *and* there is nothing too hard for thee:

Jer 32:27 Behold, I *am* the LORD, the God of all flesh: is there any thing too hard for me?

Mat 19:26 But Jesus beheld *them,* and said unto them, With men this is impossible; but with God all things are possible.

Mar 9:23 Jesus said unto him, If thou canst believe, all things *are* possible to him that believeth.

Mar 10:27 And Jesus looking upon them saith, With men *it is* impossible, but not with God: for with God all things are possible.

Mar 14:36 And he said, Abba, Father, all things *are* possible unto thee; take away this cup from me: nevertheless not what I will, but what thou wilt.

Statutes Forever - Throughout Old Testament scripture there are texts that should, perhaps, be commented upon as delicately as possible to avoid criticizing the innocent; whom ever that may be, or have been! But we must also try to state reality, which is:
The covenant promoting ***"Statutes Forever"*** have been broken time after time, after time over the centuries, and on at least two occasions God severely punished Israel because of breaking the covenant. Therefore, it seems the question that must be addressed in our day, is the following! Does the LORD God even notice anyone that tries to

do the ordinances Moses was given and then practiced with the people of Israel by Levi *(managers of the Old Testament priesthood)*? And what credit does He assign for anyone that attempts doing this? After all, that covenant has been broken: However, it is put together again in the Lord Jesus Christ and His *"Sacrificial Atoning Work"*; the New Covenant, which is unbreakable *(because it is between God the Father and God the Son)*!

But no one is qualified, nor, I believe, has the favor of God, to wag the finger in condemnation of the people God have chosen. And we know from prophetic scripture that God shall keep a remnant of this people, Israel unto Himself!

So then, is it correct to say the, *"Statutes Forever"* are collected again in the Lord Jesus Christ? I am convinced this to be the case, but you are encouraged to evaluate my assessments!

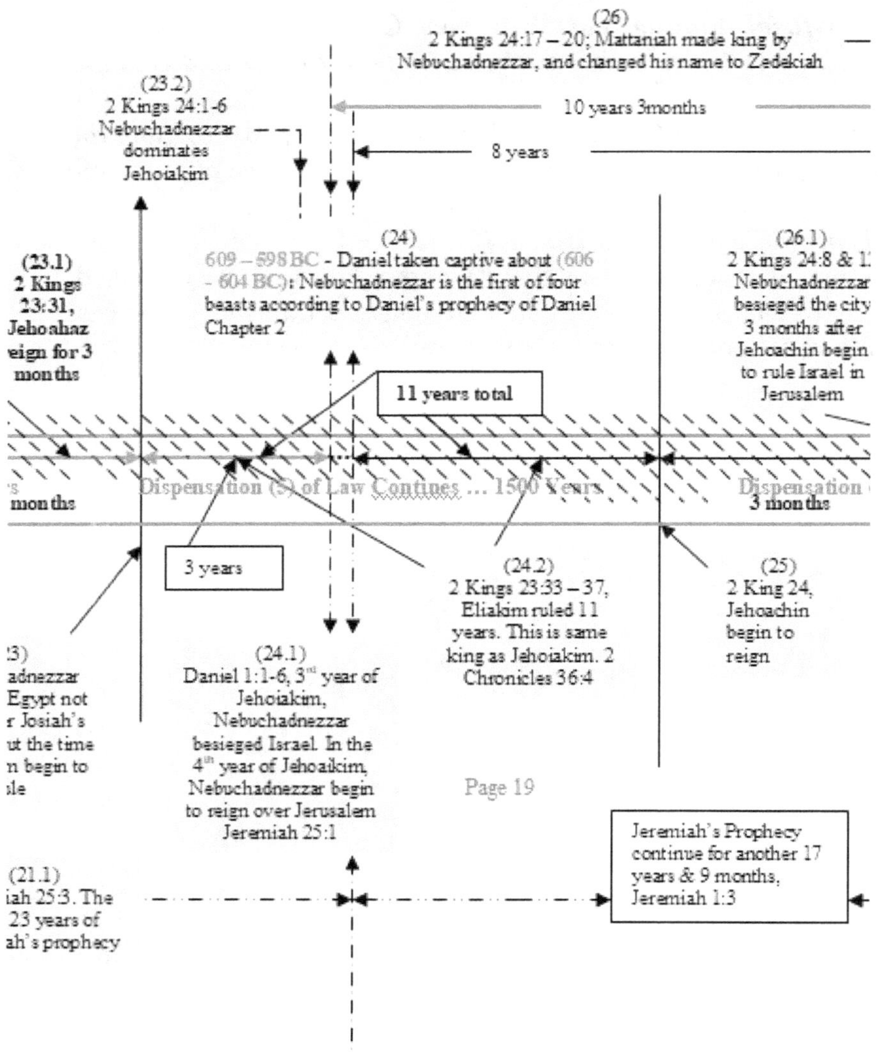
(26)
2 Kings 24:17 – 20; Mattaniah made king by Nebuchadnezzar, and changed his name to Zedekiah
(23.2)
2 Kings 24:1-6 Nebuchadnezzar dominates Jehoiakim
10 years 3months
8 years
(23.1)
2 Kings 23:31, Jehoahaz reign for 3 months
(24)
609 – 598 BC - Daniel taken captive about (606 - 604 BC): Nebuchadnezzar is the first of four beasts according to Daniel's prophecy of Daniel Chapter 2
(26.1)
2 Kings 24:8 & 1 Nebuchadnezzar besieged the city 3 months after Jehoachin begin to rule Israel in Jerusalem
11 years total
months
Dispensation (5) of Law Contines ... 1500 Years
Dispensation
3 months
3 years
(24.2)
2 Kings 23:33 – 37, Eliakim ruled 11 years. This is same king as Jehoiakim. 2 Chronicles 36:4
(25)
2 King 24, Jehoachin begin to reign
3)
adnezzar Egypt not r Josiah's ut the time n begin to le
(24.1)
Daniel 1:1-6, 3rd year of Jehoiakim, Nebuchadnezzar besieged Israel. In the 4th year of Jehoiakim, Nebuchadnezzar begin to reign over Jerusalem Jeremiah 25:1
Page 19
(21.1)
iah 25:3. The 23 years of ah's prophecy
Jeremiah's Prophecy continue for another 17 years & 9 months, Jeremiah 1:3

Two (2) Nations End: Judah of Israel Remain – Page 20
(Note: dates are approximations)

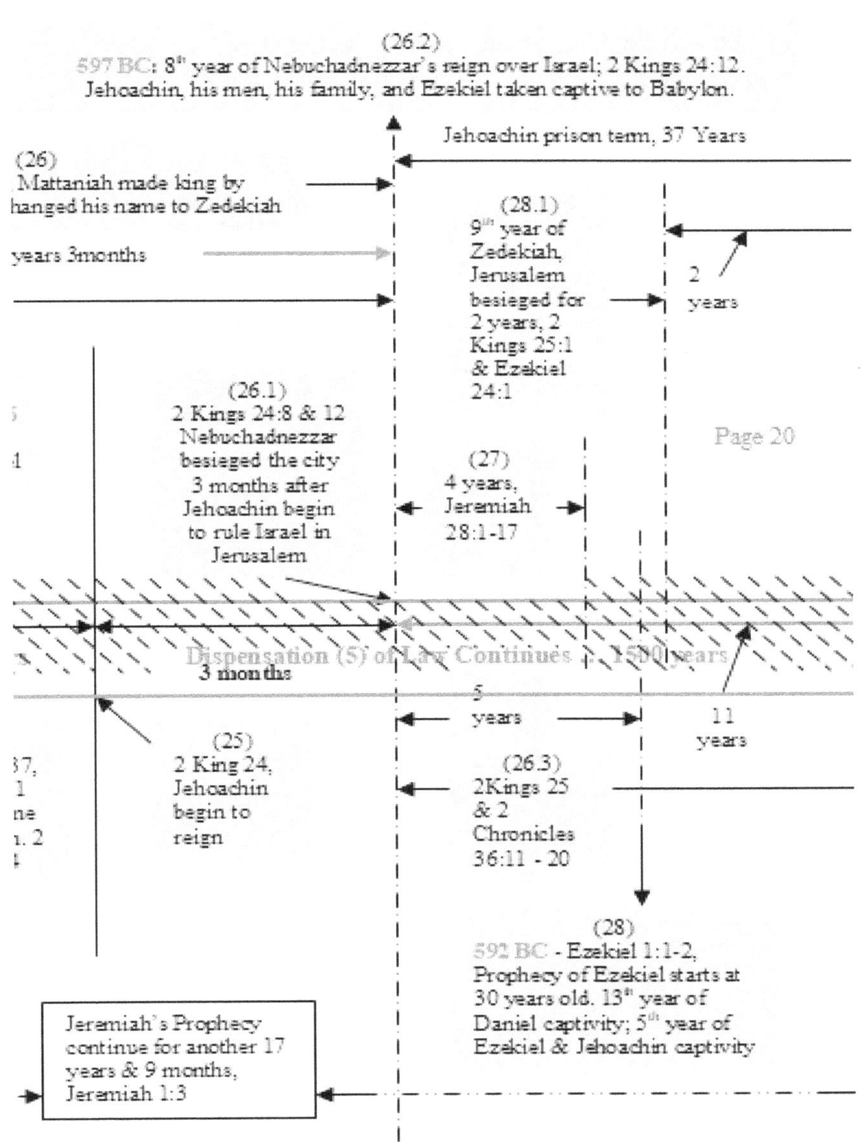

Ezra 7:1 through 7:27 presents the circumstance of complete restoration after the Temple and City has been built again. *Ezra 7:7 and 7:8* identify the period of time as beginning the seventh *(7th) year* of *Artaxerxes I*.

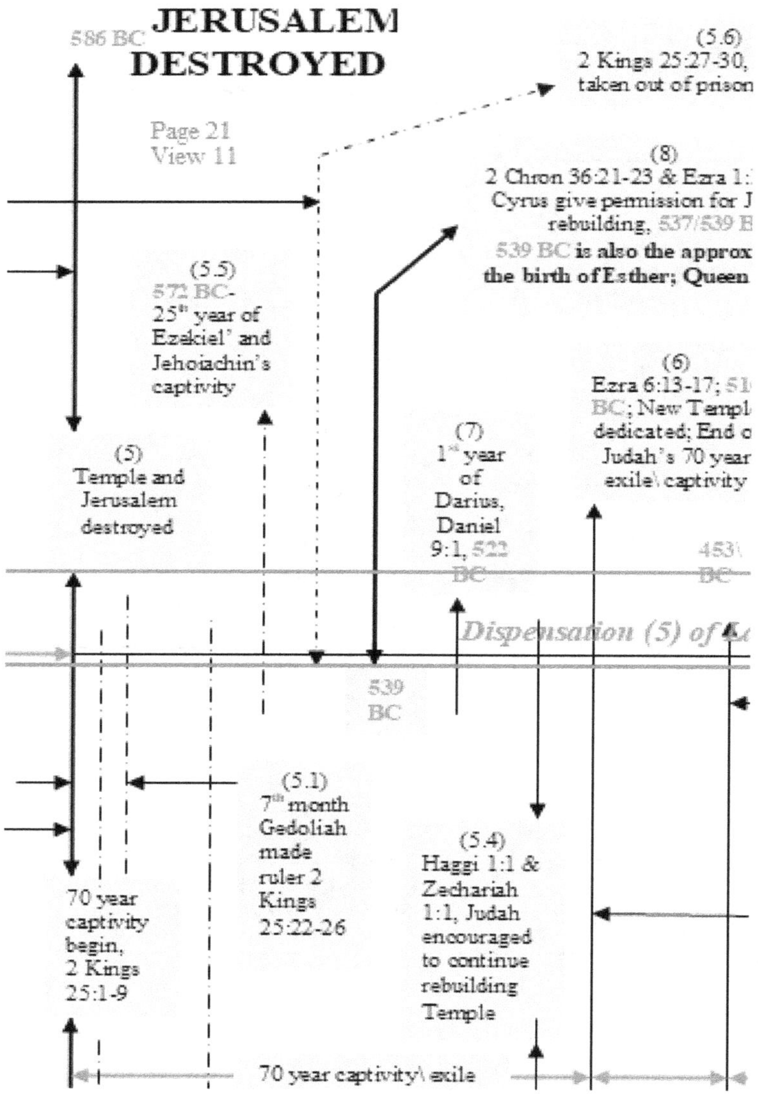

There were more than one "Artaxerxes" that ruled the *Persian Empire*, but the ruler at this time of Ezra, according to historical accounts, reigned from *464 to 425 B.C.* Thus, the *seventh (7th) year* of Artaxerxes would be *457 B.C.* This is accurate to within half *(1/2)* years of being *483 years* prior to the coming ministry of Messiah, as prophesied by *Daniel in Chapter 9 verse 25.* Given the degree of possible error that is inherent with historical dating, this is very convincing that the calendar dates referenced in this timeline illustration are quite realistic (i.e., taking into consideration the calendar corrected birth of Jesus was *4 to 6 B.C. (or 4 to 6 years earlier)*, rather than *Zero B.C.*)! *(457 B.C. – 4 – 483 = - 30, or 30 A.D.; which was the beginning of the ministry of Jesus). Daniel 9:27* prophesied that Jesus would be crucified *3 ½ to 4 years* later *(400 B.C. – 434 = - 34, or 34 A.D.)! (Note: dates are approximations)*

Two (2) Nations End: Judah of Israel Remain – Page 21 View 21
(Note: dates are approximations)

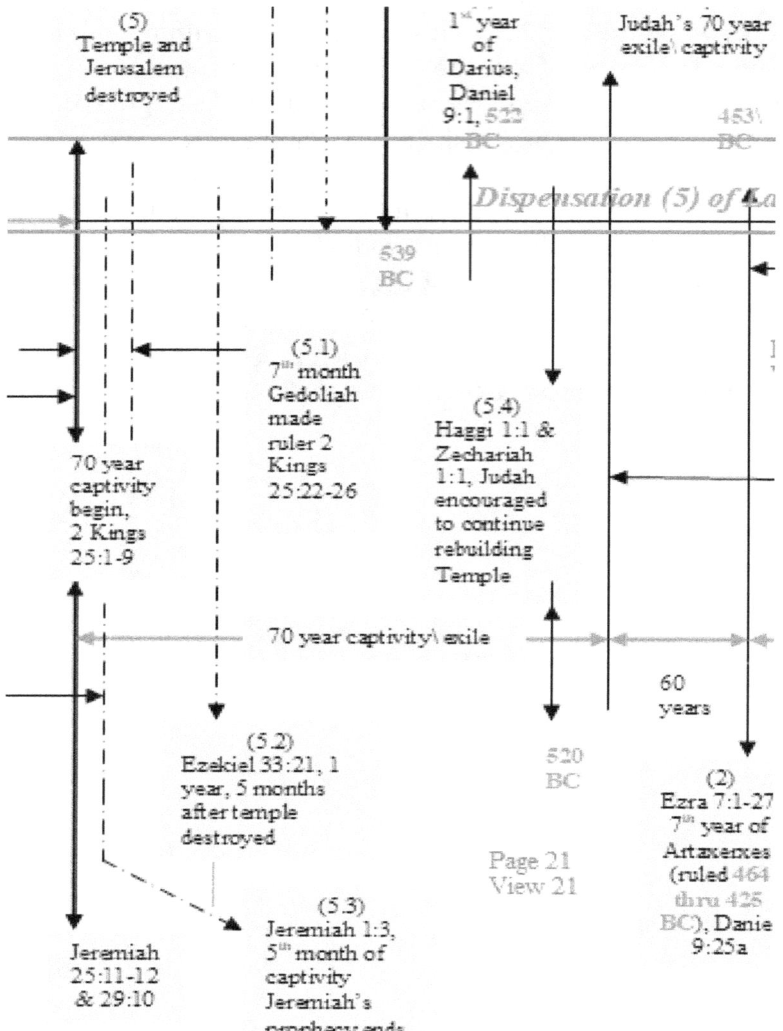

Two (2) Nations End: Judah of Israel Remain – Page 21 View 31
(Note: dates are approximations)

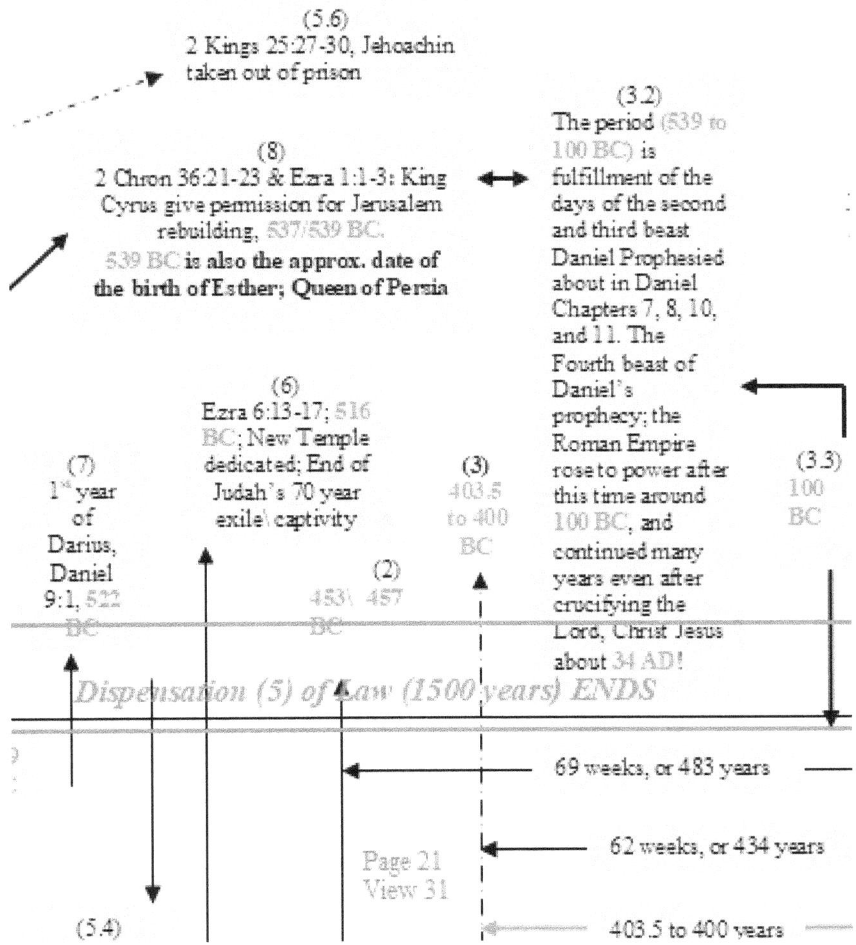

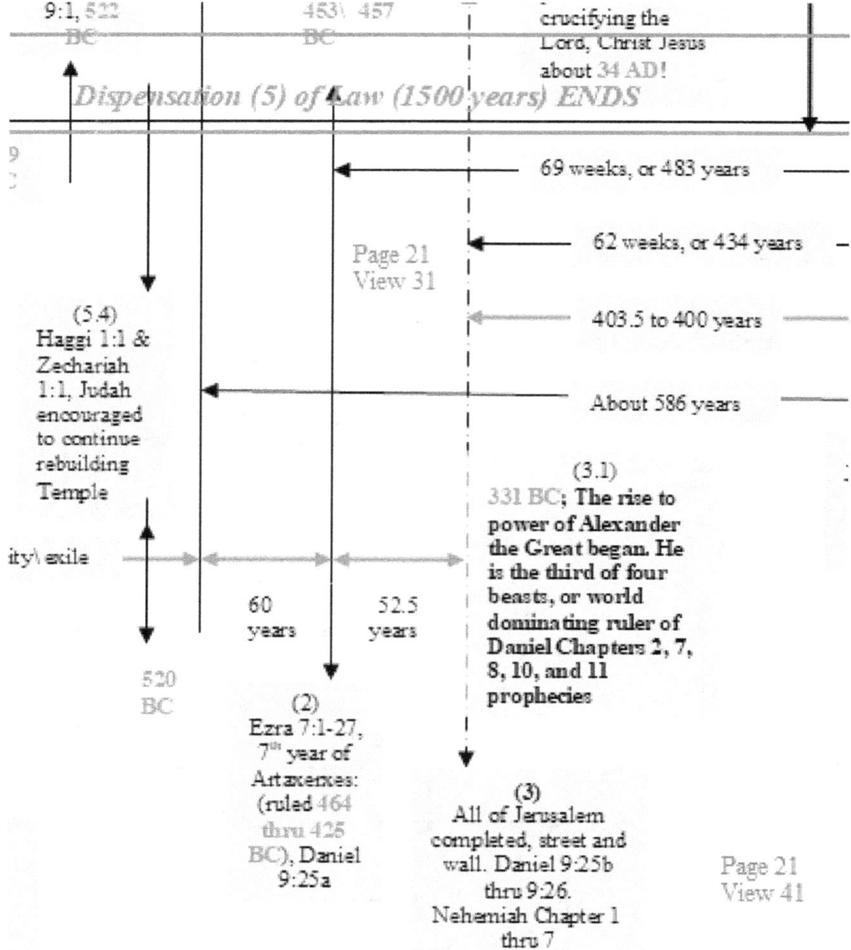
9:1, 522 BC
453\ 457 BC
crucifying the Lord, Christ Jesus about 34 AD!
Dispensation (5) of Law (1500 years) ENDS
69 weeks, or 483 years
62 weeks, or 434 years
403.5 to 400 years
About 586 years
Page 21 View 31
(5.4) Haggi 1:1 & Zechariah 1:1, Judah encouraged to continue rebuilding Temple
ity\ exile
(3.1) 331 BC; The rise to power of Alexander the Great began. He is the third of four beasts, or world dominating ruler of Daniel Chapters 2, 7, 8, 10, and 11 prophecies
520 BC
60 years
52.5 years
(2) Ezra 7:1-27, 7th year of Artaxerxes: (ruled 464 thru 425 BC), Daniel 9:25a
(3) All of Jerusalem completed, street and wall. Daniel 9:25b thru 9:26. Nehemiah Chapter 1 thru 7
Page 21 View 41

Israel's Religious Authority Rejected the Prophecy and Cornerstone; which was the First Coming of the Lord Jesus Christ, and assisted the Romans in Crucifying the Lord of glory instead:

(1) - *Luke 3:1-22:* Jesus was baptized by *John the Baptist*, and anointed with the *Holy Spirit* in the fifteenth *(15th) year* of the reign *Tiberius Caesar. (Note: dates are approximations)*

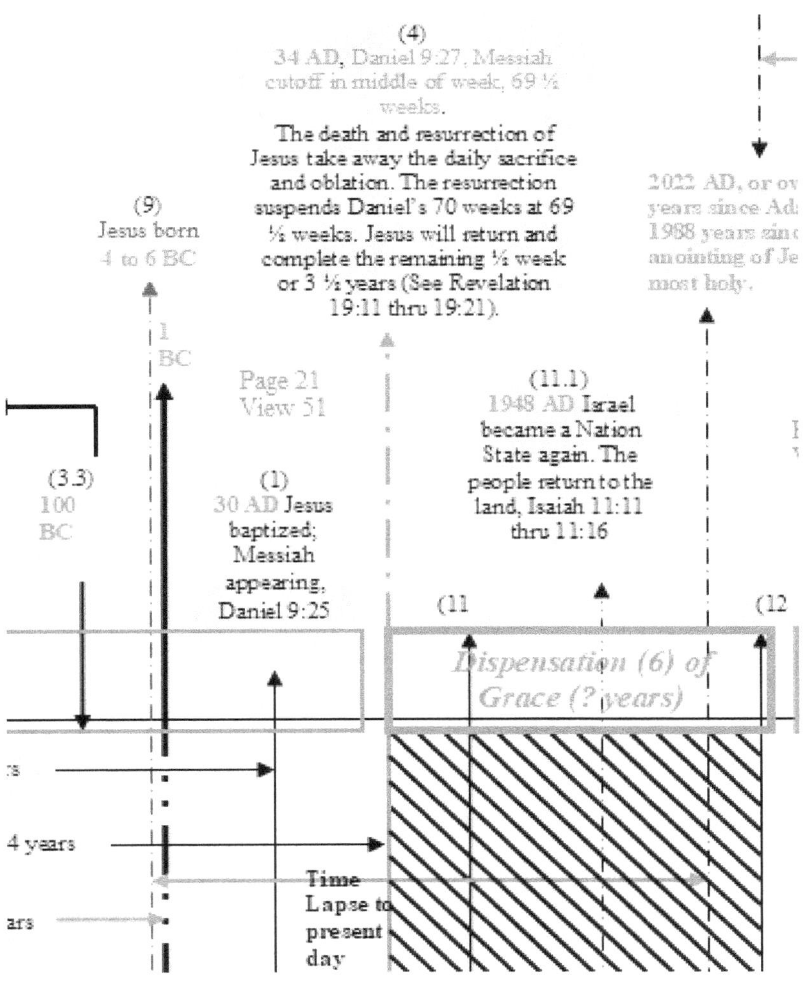

According to secular history, *Tiberius Caesar Augustus* ruled Rome from fourteen *(14) to* thirty seven *(37) A.D.* Therefore, the *15th year of Tiberius Caesar* would have been *Approx. 29, or 30 A.D. on the Julian\ Gregorian Calendar.* It is at this time that Jesus began to verify and confirm promises of God to the Jewish people according to Old Testament Prophecies. This began His three and one-half *(3 ½) year ministry.*

1- a. As *Daniel 9:25* states, "know therefore and understand that from the going forth of the command to restore and build Jerusalem unto *Messiah the Prince* shall be *seven (7) weeks, and threescore and two weeks", or 483 years*. Therefore, *483 years prior* to Jesus' baptism and anointing, at His *John the Baptist baptism,* we would anticipate seeing scripture that would fulfill a command to build and restore Jerusalem to what it was before the destruction in *586 B.C.* by King Nebuchadnezzar of Babylon. *(Note: dates are approximations)*

Two (2) Nations End: Judah of Israel Remain – Page 21 View 61
(Note: dates are approximations)

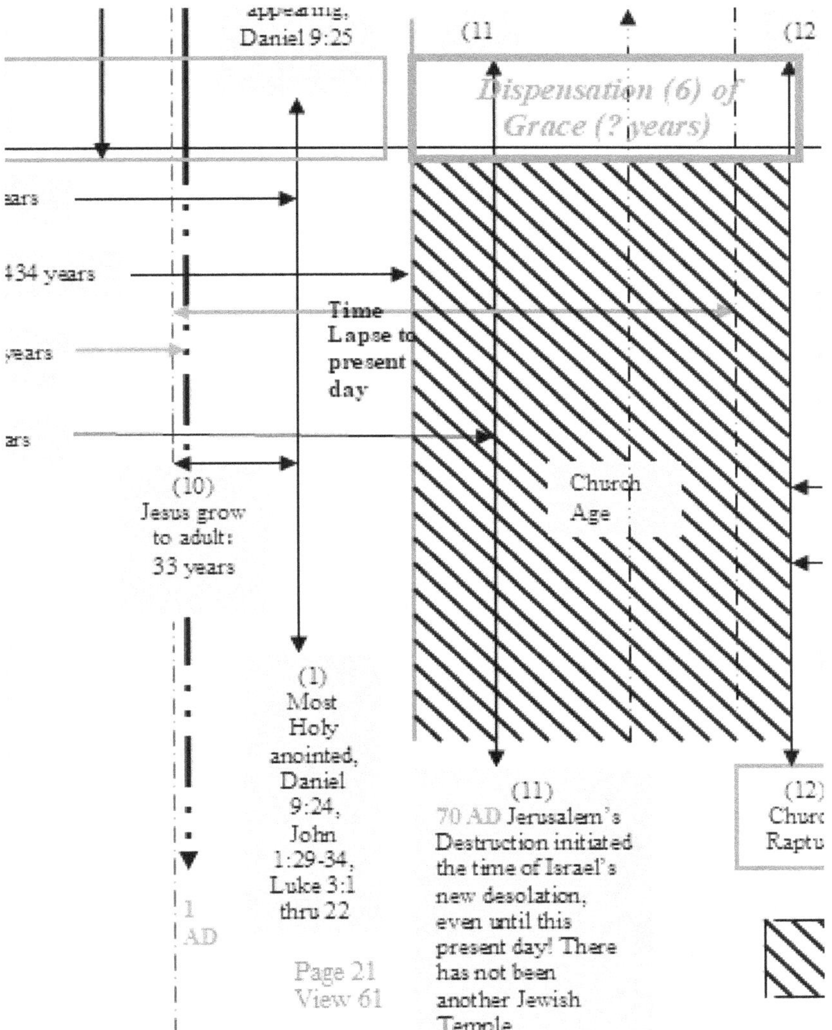

Post Resurrection Church Age – Page 22 View 1
(Note: dates are approximations)

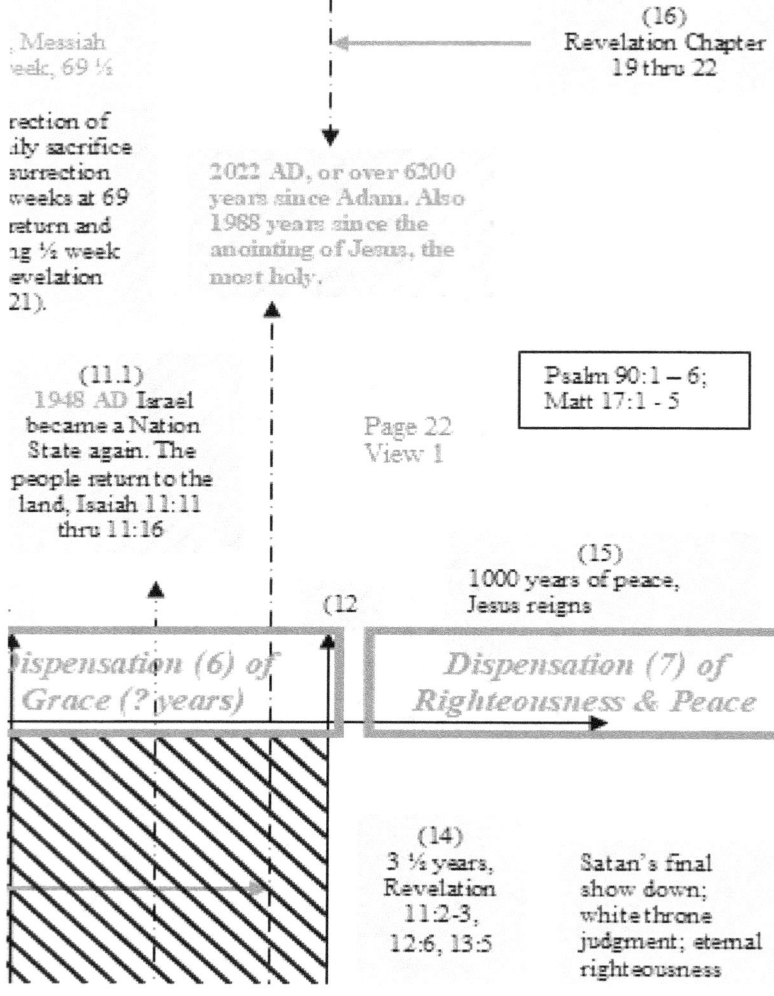

Post Resurrection Church Age – Page 22 View 2
(Note: dates are approximations)

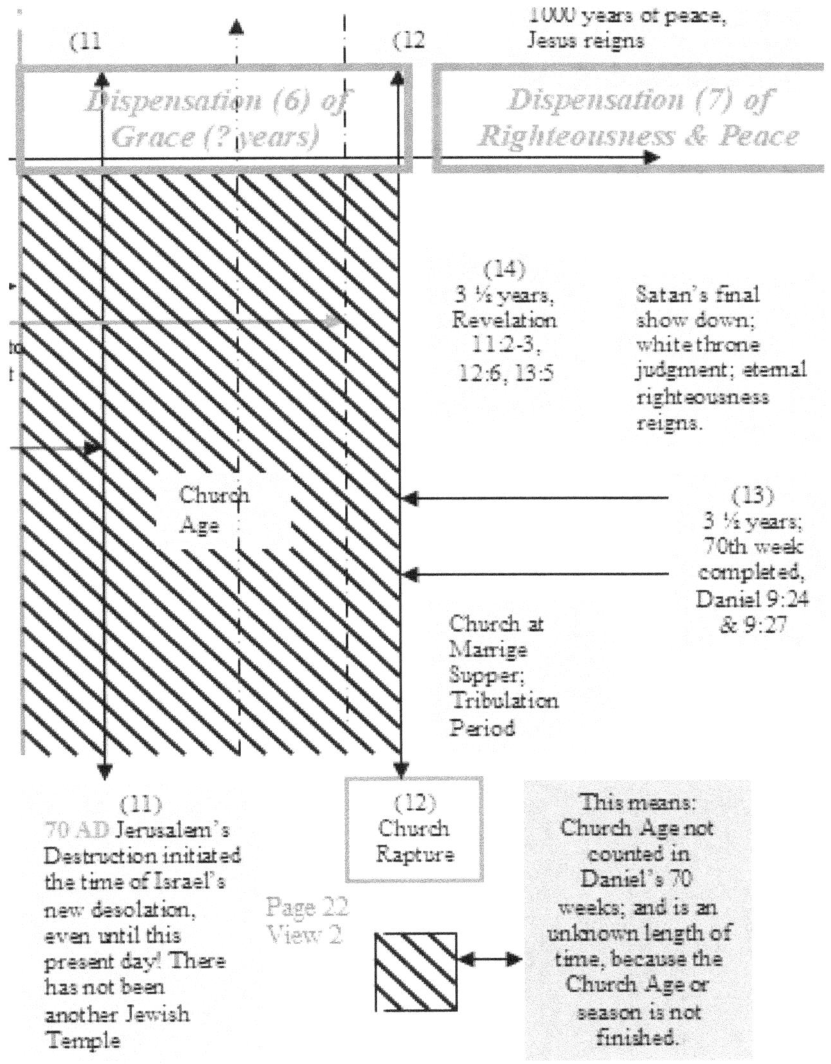

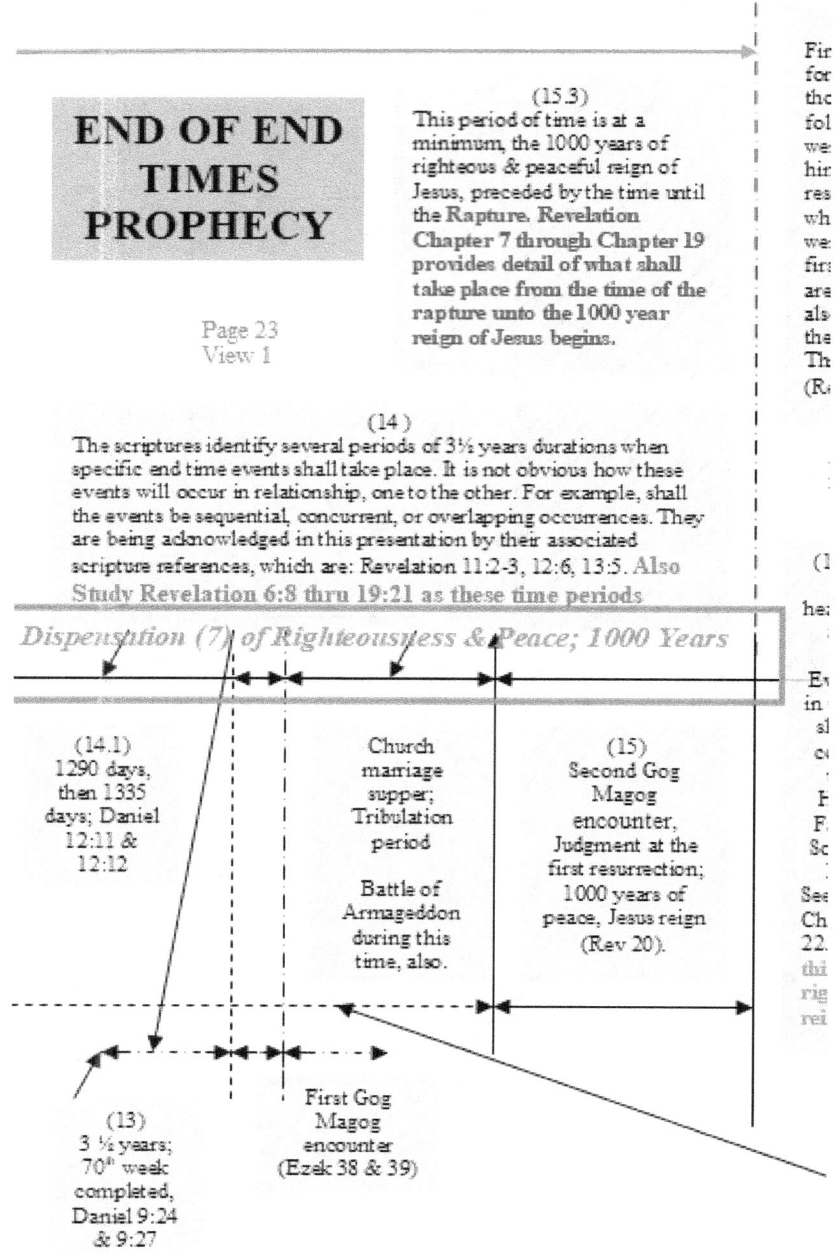

END OF END TIMES PROPHECY

Page 23
View 1

(15.3)
This period of time is at a minimum, the 1000 years of righteous & peaceful reign of Jesus, preceded by the time until the Rapture. Revelation Chapter 7 through Chapter 19 provides detail of what shall take place from the time of the rapture unto the 1000 year reign of Jesus begins.

(14)
The scriptures identify several periods of 3½ years durations when specific end time events shall take place. It is not obvious how these events will occur in relationship, one to the other. For example, shall the events be sequential, concurrent, or overlapping occurrences. They are being acknowledged in this presentation by their associated scripture references, which are: Revelation 11:2-3, 12:6, 13:5. Also Study Revelation 6:8 thru 19:21 as these time periods

Dispensation (7) of Righteousness & Peace; 1000 Years

(14.1)
1290 days, then 1335 days; Daniel 12:11 & 12:12

Church marriage supper; Tribulation period

Battle of Armageddon during this time, also.

(15)
Second Gog Magog encounter, Judgment at the first resurrection; 1000 years of peace, Jesus reign (Rev 20).

(13)
3 ½ years; 70th week completed, Daniel 9:24 & 9:27

First Gog Magog encounter (Ezek 38 & 39)

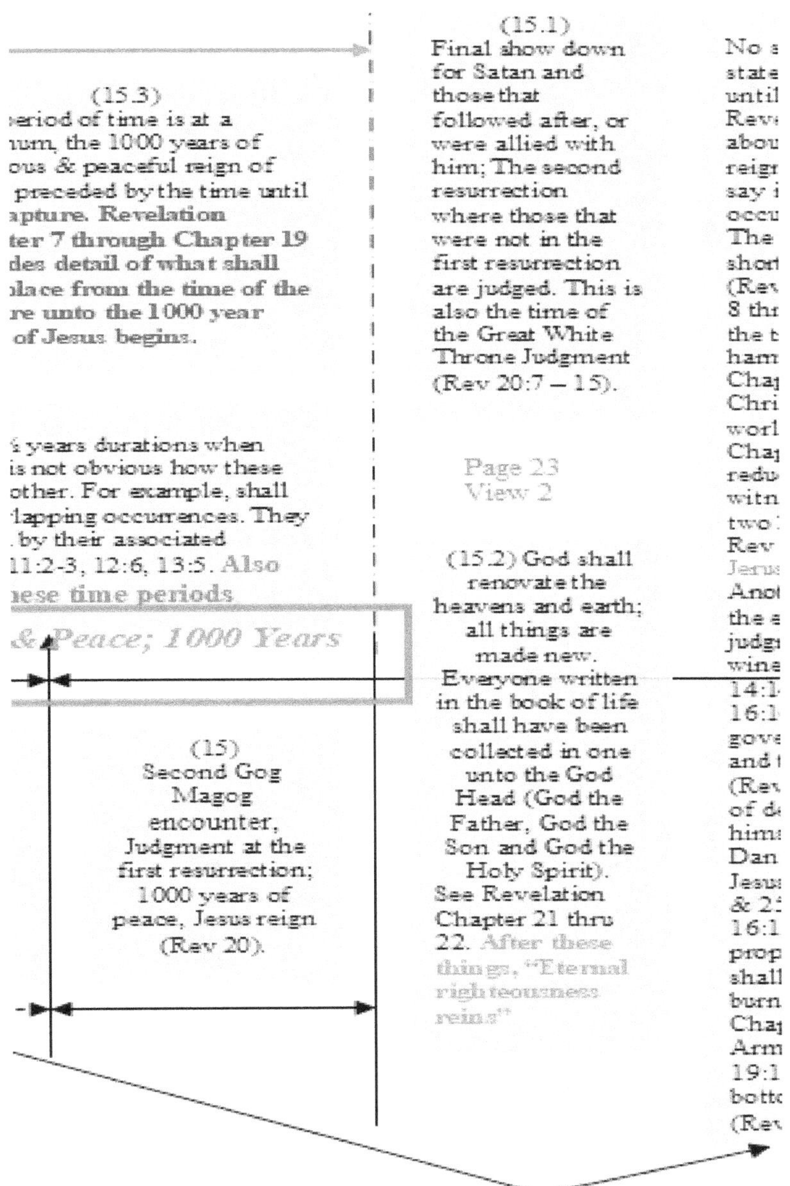
(15.3)
eriod of time is at a
um, the 1000 years of
ous & peaceful reign of
preceded by the time until
pture. Revelation
ter 7 through Chapter 19
des detail of what shall
lace from the time of the
re unto the 1000 year
of Jesus begins.

 years durations when
is not obvious how these
other. For example, shall
lapping occurrences. They
by their associated
11:2-3, 12:6, 13:5. Also
ese time periods

& Peace; 1000 Years

(15)
Second Gog
Magog
encounter,
Judgment at the
first resurrection;
1000 years of
peace, Jesus reign
(Rev 20).

(15.1)
Final show down
for Satan and
those that
followed after, or
were allied with
him; The second
resurrection
where those that
were not in the
first resurrection
are judged. This is
also the time of
the Great White
Throne Judgment
(Rev 20:7 – 15).

Page 23
View 2

(15.2) God shall
renovate the
heavens and earth;
all things are
made new.
Everyone written
in the book of life
shall have been
collected in one
unto the God
Head (God the
Father, God the
Son and God the
Holy Spirit).
See Revelation
Chapter 21 thru
22. After these
things, "Eternal
righteousness
reigns"

No s
state
until
Rev
abou
reigr
say i
occu
The
shor
(Rev
8 thr
the t
ham
Chaj
Chri
worl
Chaj
redu
witn
two :
Rev
Jesus
Anot
the a
judgi
wine
14:1
16:1
gove
and t
(Rev
of de
hims
Dan
Jesus
& 2:
16:1
prop
shall
burn
Chaj
Arm
19:1
botto
(Rev

)
down
1d

ter, or
with
econd
1
e that
the
ction
This is
1e of
/hite
gment
- 15).

i shall
: the
d earth;
s are
ew.
written
: of life
: been
in one
God
1d the
od the
od the
irit).
tion
thru
hese
ernal
ess

(14.2)
No specific length of time can be stated from the time of the rapture until Christ return according to Revelation 19:11 – 19:21, which is about the beginning of the 1000 year reign of Jesus. Most Bible Scholars say it is seven years. Prophetic occurrences shall be as follows: The 7 trumpet judgments takes place shortly after the Church is taken up (Rev 6:12 – 6:17, Rev 7:9 – 7:17, Rev 8 thru Rev 12:12); The 144,000 from the tribes of Israel shall be sealed from harm during the Tribulation (Rev Chapter 7); The man of sin or anti-Christ shall come to the position of world leader (Rev 6:1 – 6:8, Rev Chapters 12 & 13); The 24 hour day is reduced by one third (Rev. 8:12); Two witnesses shall prophesy a thousand two hundred and three score days (Rev Chapter 11), and the Temple at Jerusalem is put in place again; Another harvest of saints takes place at the end of the seven trumpet judgments, but before the great winepress of the wrath of God (Rev 14:14, thru 14:16, Rev 16:15 and Rev 16:16); The world's economies and governments (Babylon the great whore and the beast) shall suffer destructions (Rev Chapters 17 & 18); Abomination of desolation/ Man of sin declare himself God (Matt 24:15, Mark 13:14, Dan 12:11-12) Jesus second coming (Matt Chapter 24 & 25, Rev Chapter 19:11 – 19:21, Rev 16:15 & Rev16:16); The beast & false prophet is not permitted to die but shall be cast into the lake of fire burning with brimstone (Rev Chapter19:20); The Battle of Armageddon (Rev 16:12-21, Rev. 19:11-21); Satan shall be bound in the bottomless pit for a thousand years (Rev 20:1 – 3)

(16)
Eternal righteousness reins in Heaven and Earth. In that day whosoever is with God shall remain with Him forever:

THE NEW CREATION

NEW JERUSALEM; THE HEAD-QUATERS OF GOD ON EARTH

Measurements of the Holy City; New Jerusalem

The Holy City; New Jerusalem is Constructed of Precious Stones

The Holy City; New Jerusalem Shall be Filled with the Glory of God

SEE REFERENCE BOOK TEXTS & THE JUDEO – CHRISTIAN BIBLE

CREATION SHALL BE MADE NEW

Thy Throne Forever – The eternal LORD and God of Creation made this promise of his eternal kingdom to King David. But New Testament Judeo – Christian Scriptures clearly explains that corruptible can not inherit incorruptible *(1 Corinthians 15:53 through 15:55)*, because incorruptible is *"forever"*. Thus, the obvious and natural question arises; "how is this promise the LORD God gave corruptible David, possible"?

Throughout history no throne of man has continued more than a hand full of years, compared to all the time of recorded history; and the promise to David was for eternity! And so, the short answer to the question is, *"by love; grace; mercy; regeneration\ resurrection; inheritance; Kinsman Redemption; sacrifice; and … other works of the Lord Jesus Christ (Son of God 100%; son, and progeny of King David, who is 100% man)"*!

The genealogy of the Lord Jesus Christ is given in the New Testament Book of Matthew Chapter 1(one). And we see that his genealogy traces through David, the Great King of Israel; the youngest son of Jesse, as is revealed in scriptures of Ruth Chapter 4, 1 Samuel Chapter 16, and 2 Samuel Chapter 7. Thus, the flesh and blood man Jesus, Messiah traces unto the man, Adam (no demonic hybrid, of any sorts was given, and can not claim, such a genealogy); and he, the man Adam was created of God in the image of God! Study again, Genesis 1:26 and 1:27 and John 10:1 through 10:18. Thus, the genealogy is proven, according to the Word of God; without sin or contamination of any sort!

But to see the complete *(or full)* answer of sacrificing, atoning and inheritance *(of the LORD God; Jesus the Son, for his followers and believers)* we must "diligently" study both, the Old and New Testament Judeo – Christian Bible Books; which is *the Words of God given to us that we may know Him and His plans for the human race; no other document(s) provide this! Do we not see in this how the LORD God of Creation leaves nothing to chance; and who else would you suppose could maintain such precise and factual records of the centuries?*

Gen 18:14 Is any thing too hard for the LORD? At the time appointed I will return unto thee, according to the time of life, and Sarah *(at 90 years of age)* shall have a son *(Isaac)*.

Jer_32:17 Ah Lord GOD! behold, thou hast made the heaven and the earth by thy great power and stretched out arm, *and* there is nothing too hard for thee:

Jer_32:27 Behold, I *am* the LORD, the God of all flesh: is there any thing too hard for me?

Mat_19:26 But Jesus beheld *them,* and said unto them, With men this is impossible; but with God all things are possible.

Mar_9:23 Jesus said unto him, If thou canst believe, all things *are* possible to him that believeth.

Mar_10:27 And Jesus looking upon them saith, With men *it is* impossible, but not with God: for with God all things are possible.

Thus, the eternal LORD and God of Creation establish the final state of those <u>BELIEVERS</u> in Him to be eternally with God!

When Does Daniel's Prophecy of Seventy Weeks Begin & End -
Obviously more number of years *(i.e., 7 Years per Week x 70 Weeks = 490 Years)* which constitutes Daniel's prophecy of seventy *(70)* weeks have passed since their beginning at Ezra's and Nehemiah's writings! But the prophecy shall not be complete until Jesus fulfills the second (2nd) half of the final *week* of the seventy *(70)*.
The prophecy began with the rebuilding efforts of Jerusalem by Ezra and continued with the rebuilding efforts of Nehemiah. The times were *(483 years, or 69 weeks)* before the appearing and ministry of Jesus, and *(434 years, or 69 1\2 week)* before Jesus was crucified *(i.e., Daniel 9:26 says "cut off")*.
When Jesus was crucified; all but *1\2 week, or 3 1\2 years* of the prophecy was complete. But the count of *weeks* for the prophecy was suspended because the National *(or Religious)* ruling Jewish authority rejected Jesus, and persuaded the Romans to crucify Him *(Jesus\ Messiah)*!
Dispensation *(6)* of Grace and the Church Age began here unto our present time, as we anticipate the second *(2nd)* appearing of Jesus to *"Rapture the Church"*, and complete the final *1/2 week, or 3 1/2 years* of Daniel, and Revelation's Prophecies!

When anyone understand Daniel and his prophecies it becomes clear why Jesus spoke specifically of Daniel in His teaching of what's expected concerning future events.
Daniel Chapter 12 provides a summary of Apostle John's Book of Revelation!

INDEX OF TIMELINE REFERENCES

Commentary of Specific Points on the Timeline

Note: The number in parentheses ( ) corresponds to that on the Timeline Illustration(s), and POINT TO the commentary below that explains the circumstances at the particular point in time on the timeline. Also be aware that the timeline dates are calculated approximations with Commentary **(1); baptism of Jesus by John the Baptist** being the reference point.

Josiah inherited the rule over Judah after Amon his father was killed:
(20, 21, 21.1, 22) – Josiah was eight years old when he began to reign in Judah thirty one years. He did that which was right in the sight of the LORD by removing idol worship, and he walked in all the way of David his father (2Kings 22:1 through 2Kings 23:30). Jeremiah began his prophecy during the thirteenth year of Josiah's reign, and continued until the fifth month after the Temple and Jerusalem was destroyed in 586 B.C. (Jeremiah 1:2 and 3).

It is about this time after the reign of Josiah that Nebuchadnezzar begin to assert his dominance in world affairs. He defeated Egypt, took authority over kings of Judah, and carried captives and spoils back to Babylon, as it pleased him:
(23, 23.1, 23.2) – The people of Judah took Jehoahaz the son of Josiah, and anointed him, and made him king in his father's place. He did that which was evil in the sight of God, and he only reigned three months, because Egypt took him captive back to Egypt; put the nation to tribute of a hundred talent of silver and a talent of gold. Jehoahaz died in Egypt. Egypt also made Eliakim, the son Josiah king in Judah, and changed his name to Jehoiakim. Jehoiakim/Eliakim was twenty five years old when he began to reign; and he reigned eleven years (2Kings 23:31 through 23:37).

The captivity of Daniel and the three Hebrew boys (Shadrach, Meshaach, and Abednego) began in the third year of the reign of Jehoiakim/Eliakim:
(24, 24.1, 24.2) – Daniel 1:1 through 6: In the third year of the reign of Jehoiakim/Eliakim Daniel and the Hebrew boys were among the captives that Nebuchadnezzar took from Judah. This was also about the time Jehoiakim/Eliakim rebelled against Nebuchadnezzar (2Kings 24:1). Then, in the fourth year of Jehoaikim/Eliakim Nebuchadnezzar begin his conquering reign over Judah (Jeremiah 25:1). Jehoiakim/Eliakim reigned eleven years, did that which was evil in the sight of God, and then his son Jehoiachin reigned in Judah/Jerusalem after him.

Jehoiachin was eighteen years old when he began to reign, and after he reigned in Jerusalem three months Nebuchadnezzar king of Babylon, once again, came up against Jerusalem and besieged it:
(25, 26, 26.1, 26.2) – Jehoiachin did that which was evil in the sight of Lord, according to all that his father did. (2Kings 24:11through 17) And Nebuchadnezzar king of Babylon came against the city, and his servants did besiege it. And Jehoiachin the king of Judah went out to the king of Babylon, he, and his mother, and his servants, and his princes, and his officers: and the king of Babylon took him in the eighth year of his reign. And he carried out thence all the treasures of the house of the LORD, and the treasures of the king's house, and cut in pieces all the vessels of gold which Solomon king of Israel had made in the temple of the LORD, as the LORD had said. And he carried away all Jerusalem, and all the princes, and all the mighty men of valour, even ten thousand captives, and all the craftsmen and smiths: none remained, save the poorest sort of the people of the land. And he carried away Jehoiachin to Babylon, and the king's mother, and the king's wives, and his

officers, and the mighty of the land, those carried he into captivity from Jerusalem to Babylon. And all the men of might, even seven thousand, and craftsmen and smiths a thousand, all that were strong and apt for war, even them the king of Babylon brought captive to Babylon. **And the king of Babylon** *(Nebuchadnezzar)* **made Mattaniah** *(Jehoiachin's)* **father's brother king in his stead, and changed his name to Zedekiah. Zedekiah was twenty one years old when he began to reign, and he reigned eleven years in Jerusalem:**
(26.3, 27, 28, 28.1) – Zedekiah did that which was evil in the sight of the LORD, according to all that Jehoiakim had done. For through the anger of the LORD it came to pass in Jerusalem and Judah, until he had cast them out from his presence, that Zedekiah rebelled against the king of Babylon. Jerusalem and the temple was destroyed at this time in 586 B.C. (2Kings Chapter 25).

---- JERUSALEM DESTROYED - 586 B.C. Through Book of Revelation ----
Israel Rejected the Prophecy and Cornerstone; the First Coming of the Lord Jesus Christ, and assisted the Romans in Crucifying the Lord of glory instead:
(1) - Luke 3:1-22: Jesus was baptized by John the Baptist, and anointed with the *Holy Spirit* in the 15th year of the reign Tiberius Caesar.
According to secular history, Tiberius Caesar Augustus ruled Rome from 14 to 37 A.D. Therefore, the 15th year of Tiberius Caesar would be Approx. 29, or 30 A.D. It is at this time that Jesus began to confirm God's promises to the Jewish people. This began his 3 ½ year ministry.
1-a. As Daniel 9:25 states "know therefore and understand that from the going forth of the command to restore and build Jerusalem unto Messiah the Prince shall be seven weeks, and threescore and two weeks", or 483 years. Therefore, 483 years prior to Jesus' baptism and anointing we would anticipate seeing scripture that would fulfill a command to build and restore Jerusalem to what it was before the destruction in 586 B.C. by King Nebuchadnezzar of Babylon.
(2) - Ezra 7:1-27 seem to meet all the conditions of *"1-a"* above more than any other scriptures.
There were several stages in the rebuilding process of Jerusalem. The people would build for a while, and lose heart, or meet opposition from neighboring communities. Then, they would need to be encouraged (commanded) to continue the building effort all over again. Ezra 7:1- 27 presents the circumstance of complete restoration after the Temple and City has been built. *Ezra 7:7 and 7:8* identify the period of time as the *7th year* of *Artaxerxes I.* There were more than one "Artaxerxes" that ruled, but the ruler at this time of Ezra, according to historical accounts, reigned from *464 to 425 B.C.* Thus, the *seventh (7th) year* of Artaxerxes would be *457 B.C.* This is accurate to within half *(1/2)* years of being *483 years* prior to the coming ministry of Messiah, as prophesied by *Daniel in Chapter 9 verse 25.* Given the degree of possible error that is inherent with historical dating, this is very convincing that the calendar dates used in this timeline illustration are quite realistic (i.e., taking into consideration the calendar corrected birth of Jesus was *4 to 6 B.C. (or 4 to 6 years earlier)*, rather than *Zero B.C.*)! *(457 B.C. – 4 – 483 = - 30, or 30 A.D.; which was the beginning of the ministry of Jesus). Daniel 9:27* shows us that Jesus was crucified *3 ½ to 4 years* later *(400 B.C. – 434 = - 34, or 34 A.D.)!*

(3, 3.1, 3.2) - All of Jerusalem has been completed; including street and wall (see the last line of Daniel 9:25, and the first line of Daniel 9:26).
We see in Nehemiah Chapter 1 through 7, preparations, and the final stage of building the city wall. Nehemiah Chapter 2 verse 1 identifies the point in time as the 20th year of Artaxerxes. It is believed that this is the same *Artaxerxes I* encountered in Ezra 7:1-27,

because he ruled from 464 to 425 B.C. Thus, Artaxerxes' 20th year would be 444 B.C. With the information that is available, it is not known how long after this final building effort that the 62 weeks of Daniel 9:26 began. But we know the 62 weeks ended (4) 3 ½-years or ½-week after Messiah's coming/ministry began (1), which is (29 A.D. + 3 ½) = 32 ½ -A.D. Therefore, 434 years prior to 32 ½-A.D. is the year 403 ½ -B.C. (3). Also apply analysis of **(1) and (2)** above!

The Church Age Begins:
(4) - The end of Daniel's 62 weeks, or 434 years is also the point of the crucifixion and resurrection of Christ Jesus, the beginning of the Church Age, and Daniel's 70 weeks are suspended at 69 ½ weeks until the Book of Revelation when the remaining ½ week (or 3 ½ years) shall be completed. Messiah was cut-off in the middle of the week, but not for himself.

Judah's 70 Years of Captivity:
(5, 5.1, 5.2, 5.3, 5.4, 5.5, 5.6) - The official beginning of Judah's captivity when the Temple was destroyed in 586 B.C. Nebuchadnezzar came against Jerusalem at other times before this final destruction. Daniel was taken captive during one of those earlier times *(about 605 B.C.)*, along with others, including Shadrach, Meshach and Abednego.

(6) - The rebuilt Temple at Jerusalem was dedicated 70 years after the destruction in 586 B.C. 70 years was the period of Judah's captivity as prophesied by Jeremiah 25:11-12, and Jeremiah 29:10.
Ezra 6:13-17 says the Temple was dedicated in the 6th year of Darius. Upon investigating historical dates about this Darius prior to the time of Ezra, (since secular history records identify more than one Darius) it was determined that this Darius began to reign in 522 B.C. (7). Therefore, the 6th year of his reign would be 516 B.C.
Thus, (586 B.C. – 70-years = 516 B.C.). Bible Scholars and teachers refer to this temple as "Zerubbabel's Temple." Also, King Herod later remodeled it as part of his efforts of building improvements to Jerusalem, during his reign under Rome.
(7) - The 1st year *(522 B.C.)* of the reign of that Darius discussed in Ezra 6:13-17 is in fact referring back to the same Darius of 516 B.C. Six years later was the end of Judah's 70 years of captivity.

(8) - At the height of the 2nd world empire, which was Medo-Persia, (see Daniel Chapter 2, 7 and 8) "Cyrus The Great" being ruler; a record was established that opened the way for Jerusalem to be rebuilt. This was about the year 537-539 B.C. Scripture references for this event is 2 Chronicles 36:21-23, and Ezra 1:1-3.

When was Jesus Born?
(9) - The estimated date of the birth of Christ Jesus; between 4 and 6 B.C.
At one time historians put Christ's birth at Zero B.C. But it was later re-calculated to be "4 to 6 B.C." perhaps because it was determined that Herod The Great died about or before 4 B.C. In the Gospels of Matthew, Mark, and Luke, Herod the Great is a very present individual, as king in Jerusalem, before and after the birth of Jesus. Thus, it is quite unlikely for Jesus to have been born in Zero B.C., which is 4 years after Herod's death.

(10) - Approximate number of years (27 to 33) from Christ's birth to his anointing with the Holy Ghost; which is also when he was baptized by John The Baptist, and began his ministry; Fulfilling of Daniel 9:24, "The Most Holy anointed". I have heard it said that the

Most Holy is the temple, but how can that be true since the temple & priesthood is a figure of Jesus communicating\ interceding with God for men?

Jerusalem Destroyed by the Roman Empire:
(11, 11.1) - Jerusalem and the Temple were destroyed once again, this time by the Romans in 70 A.D.
The Jewish people became scattered throughout the nation of the world until 1948 A.D. At that time, after World War II, the Americans and Allied Forces were key in support of Israel becoming an organized state again. But the desolation of having no place of worship has continued since 70 A.D. Present day circumstances are that the Muslims occupy part of Jerusalem and Israel occupy what's left.
For centuries the Jewish people have had no access to the Temple Mount where they once worshiped in Solomon's Temple, and the 2nd temple called Zerubbabel's Temple that was later refurbished by Herod The Great for the time that Jesus would come. This desolation is the condition spoken of in Daniel 9:26, which say, "and unto the end of war desolations are determined."

Rapture of the Church and End Time Revelation Events:
(12) - The Rapture; an event that Christians look forward to, because it will be the time of total redemption for those saved in Christ Jesus. For many this will be the first face-to-face encounter with the redeemer (Christ Jesus). The spirit of a person was made new at the believing and confession of Christ Jesus as Lord and Savior. Now, the rapture is that time when the flesh will also be converted, and the redeemed of Jesus Christ can see God face-to-face without being consumed of his Holy Fire. Critics and unbelievers may say that there is no such word as "rapture" in scripture; but the concept of the rapture, or being caught up from the earth is discussed in a number of places (1 Thes 4:7, 1 Cor 15:35-55, 2 Cor 12:2-4). And that is the meaning of "The Rapture." This event will also mark the end of the Church Age, as we currently understand it.

The Final ½ Week of Daniels 70 Weeks Must be Completed:
(13) - This is the final ½-week (3 ½-years) of Daniel's 70 weeks. Remember, Jesus was cut-off in the middle of the 1-week period he was suppose to confirm the covenant, thus he only completed 3 ½-years. See the first sentence of Daniel 9:26 and 9:27.
My presumption is that this final 3 ½-years, as shown on the timeline illustration, is not included with the Church Age, but takes place after the rapture. The timeline illustration presents this period outside of the Church Age for the sake of clarity also.
Most interpretations of scripture about events immediately following the Church Age, or rapture, seem to imply that there will be a period of 7 years in which tribulation events will occur. Revelation 11:2-3, 12:6, and 13:5 identifies several events that will play out in a period of 3 ½-years. But there is no definite indications as to how these events will occur in relationship one to the other. For example, will they occur, as sequential events as presented in scripture, will they occur within the same 3 ½-year time period, or will they overlap somehow ?
I suspect that Bible teachers specify 7 years (1 week) for the tribulation period because they ascribe Daniel 9:27 to the man of sin (or anti-christ), specifically. In the last three verses, at the end of Chapter 9, where the text explains Daniel 9:27, my view is that Messiah is the subject of the discussion, and not the man of sin.

Tribulations Resulting from the Righteous Judgment of God upon the World, Satan & His Followers, and the Earth:
(14, 14.1, 14.2) - Events that will be part of, or associated with, the tribulation period as presented in the Book of Revelation. Whatsoever the duration of this period; (3 ½-years, 7

years, or 12 years) it will be a time of exceeding great distress for inhabitants on earth. Scripture does not specifically say how long this period will be, but it does say that except the Lord shorten those days, no flesh should be saved (Matt 24:22, and Mark 13:20).

(15) - The righteousness & peaceful millennial (1000 years) reign of Christ Jesus on earth. See Revelation Chapter 20:1-6.

(16) - Absolute and final judgment, followed by eternal righteousness. See Revelation 20:7 through 22:21

Previous Writings:
- King James Version of the Bible
- Author's Previously Published Works
  - A Testimony of Jesus; Messiah, Son of the Living God. Published, Dec. 30, 2013:

    https://www.amazon.com/s?k=jimmie+jennings&i=stripbooks&ref=nb_sb_noss_1

  - Separation From God Has NO Victory; But the Invitation of John 3:16 Remains, July 2014:

  - Gog Magog, and Armageddon; Origins of End Time Battles, Men; and Judgments of God, April 2014:

  - A Testimony of Jesus 2; His Abundant Love, Work, and Prophecy, Sept 2014:

  - A Study of John's Revelation; End of Kingdoms Ruled by Men, Sept 2014:

  - A Testimony of Jesus 3: Jesus in the Pages of Genesis, March 2015:

  - A Testimony of Jesus 4: Jesus and His Disciples (Harvesting Fields 1), June 2015:

  - A Testimony of Jesus 5: Jesus and His Disciples (Harvesting Fields 2), June 2015:

  - A Testimony of Jesus 6: O Jerusalem, Jerusalem (Jeremiah in Perils), August 2015:

  - A Testimony of Jesus 7: O Jerusalem, Jerusalem (Daniel; Visions and Dreams), September 2015:

  - A Testimony of Jesus 8: O Jerusalem, Jerusalem (Ezekiel's; Visions), January 2016:

- A Testimony of Jesus 9: The Word of God for every Creature, March 2016:

- A Testimony of Jesus 10: Judah after Babylonian Exile End, April 2016:

- A Testimony of Jesus 11: God Called and Used Moses Mightily (Exodus), June 2016:

- A Testimony of Jesus 12: God Called and Used Moses Mightily (The Mosaic Law & Levi), September 2016:

- A Testimony of Jesus 13: God Called and Used Moses Mightily (Moses Number' Israel), November 2016:

- A Testimony of Jesus 14: God Called and Used Moses Mightily (Deuteronomy), March 2017:

- A Testimony of Jesus 15: God Called and Used <u>JOSHUA</u> to Walk After Moses, April 2017:

- A Testimony of Jesus 16: Jesus among the Pages of Job, April 2017:

- A Testimony of Jesus 17: Evaluating Israel: The Books of Judges and Ruth, June 2017:

- A Testimony of Jesus 18: 1 & 2 Samuel (Thy Throne Forever I), September 2017:

- A Testimony of Jesus: 1 & 2 Kings (Thy Throne Forever II), April 2018:

- A Timeline & Testimony of Jesus (Thy Throne Forever III), May 2018:

- ISAIAH & A Testimony of Jesus (Thy Throne Forever IV), June 2018:

- A Testimony of Jesus: with the Holy Spirit (Thy Throne Forever V), July 2018:

- 1 & 2 Chronicles & A Testimony of Jesus (Thy Throne Forever VI), August 2018:

- Prophetic RECORDS & A Testimony of Jesus (Thy Throne Forever VII), November 2018:

- A Testimony of Jesus, His Purpose His Invitation (Thy Throne Forever VIII), January 2019:

- A Testimony of Jesus, The Witness the Task and Transfiguration, August 2019:

- A Testimony of Jesus, THE PSALMS, August 2019:

- A Testimony of Jesus, Writings of Solomon, August 2019:
  https://www.amazon.com/Testimony-Jesus-Writings-Solomon/dp/1951469739/ref=sr_1_2?dchild=1&keywords=jimmie+jennings&qid=1600774770&s=books&sr=1-2

  OR

  https://www.amazon.com/Testimony-Jesus-Writings-Solomon/dp/168639554X/ref=sr_1_3?keywords=Jimmie+Jennings&qid=1566586684&s=gateway&sr=8-3

- Testimony of Jesus: Unbroken Timeline & Covenants of God (Volume I), October 2020:
  https://www.amazon.com/Testimony-Jesus-Unbroken-Timeline-Covenants/dp/B08MN3GJB7/ref=sr_1_36?dchild=1

&keywords=jimmie+jennings&qid=1609472998&s=books&sr=1-36

- o Testimony of Jesus: Unbroken Timeline & Covenants of God (Volume II), December 2020: https://www.amazon.com/Testimony-Jesus-Unbroken-Timeline-Covenants/dp/B08R69ZJ7S/ref=sr_1_40?dchild=1&keywords=jimmie+jennings&qid=1609472998&s=books&sr=1-40

- o Testimony of Jesus: Unbroken Timeline & Covenants of God (Volume III), December 2020: https://www.amazon.com/Testimony-Jesus-Unbroken-Timeline-Covenants/dp/B08RLVZXG5/ref=sr_1_38?dchild=1&keywords=jimmie+jennings&qid=1609472998&s=books&sr=1-38

- o Testimony of Jesus: Unbroken Timeline & Covenants of God (Volume IV), January 2021: https://www.amazon.com/Testimony-Jesus-Unbroken-Timeline-Covenants/dp/B08S2VRH8B/ref=sr_1_6?dchild=1&keywords=jimmie+jennings&qid=1614118124&s=books&sr=1-6

- o Testimony of Jesus: Unbroken Timeline & Covenants of God (Volume V), January 2021: https://www.amazon.com/Testimony-Jesus-Unbroken-Timeline-Covenants/dp/B08SGJNN7D/ref=sr_1_5?dchild=1&keywords=jimmie+jennings&qid=1614118239&s=books&sr=1-5

- o Separation From God Has NO Victory; But the Invitation of John 3:16 Remains; EDITION 2, March 2021: https://www.amazon.com/dp/B08XKYGP9N

- o A Testimony of Jesus, His Purpose His Invitation (Thy Throne Forever VIII) EDITION 2, October 2021: https://www.amazon.com/Testimony-Jesus-Purpose-Invitation-Forever-ebook/dp/B09HZPYF2R/ref=sr_1_49?keywords=jimmie+jennings&qid=1646683185&s=books&sr=1-49

  - o A Testimony of Jesus, THE PSALMS EDITION 2, October 2021: https://www.amazon.com/Testimony-Jesus-PSALMS-2-ebook/dp/B09J6MNPZX/ref=sr_1_40?keywords=jimmie+jennings&qid=1646682756&s=books&sr=1-40

  - o A Testimony of Jesus, The Witness the Task and Transfiguration EDITION 2, December 2021: https://www.amazon.com/Testimony-Jesus-Witness-Task-Transfiguration/dp/B09MYRCXH4/ref=sr_1_99?keywords=jimmie+jennings&qid=1646682112&s=books&sr=1-99

- My Website – https://www.jkejennings-author.com/
- Specific articles on My Website
  - o Where is Mount Sinai Really
  - o Revelation Against Error III
  - o Stoned for Mysteries of Jesus
  - o Blasphemy of the Holy Spirit
  - o LORD God Not Done With Israel
  - o Answering ECCLESASTES' Vanity
  - o Creation Has Cycles of Event_PRT2
  - o Kingdom of Heaven Material
  - o Biblical Seasons of Events
  - o Where God placed His Name
  - o Where God Placed His Name 1 – 2
  - o The Church Expecting the Rapture
  - o The Catholic Magnificat
  - o Review of Covenants

- o   Forgiveness and Faith
- o   Mystery Of Israel
- o   Daniel On World Kingdoms
- o   Factual Occurrences Of Prophecy
- o   Resurrection Life Only Flow From Jesus
- o   The Resurrection Rapture Of Saints
- o   Books on Creation & Dispensations
- o   NoteCells of Bible Prophecies of Jesus
- o   Others, take a look!